THE MINOR PROPHETS

THE
MINOR PROPHETS

by
Jack P. Lewis

BAKER BOOK HOUSE
Grand Rapids, Michigan

CONTENTS

Chapter I. The Minor Prophets—Why Bother? . . . 7

Chapter II. The Prophet Amos . . . 16

Chapter III. The Prophet Hosea . . . 24

Chapter IV. The Prophet Micah . . . 32

Chapter V. The Prophet Jonah . . . 39

Chapter VI. The Prophet Zephaniah . . . 46

Chapter VII. The Prophet Nahum . . . 53

Chapter VIII. The Prophet Habakkuk . . . 60

Chapter IX. The Prophet Haggai . . . 67

Chapter X. The Prophet Zechariah . . . 74

Chapter XI. The Prophet Malachi . . . 82

Chapter XII. The Prophet Obadiah . . . 89

Chapter XIII. The Prophet Joel . . . 97

Chapter I

THE MINOR PROPHETS—
WHY BOTHER?

Some years ago a Draft official said to me, "You are the people that throw away the Old Testament." I quickly denied the accusation, but in general for all we know about the minor prophets, we might as well have thrown them away. These lessons are presented in the hope that they may convince the student that he has robbed himself of his birthright by his neglect of this part of Scripture—that indeed "the things written aforetime were written for our learning" (Rom. 15:4).

There are still those who think that by diligent search they may find in advance in the prophets what they will read in the papers tomorrow. They search for automobiles, atomic bombs, airplanes, tire rationing, and the rise of world dictators. Such persons are bound to be disappointed with the lessons in this book for this author is convinced that they read these things into the prophets instead of out of them. He is convinced that this approach is a frame of mind that tends to blind the student to the true and lasting values in the prophets. It leaves the prophet's message a puzzle to the prophet's hearers rather than being a revelation to them.

The church fathers were interested in the prophets for their "testimony" value. That is, they sought proof texts which by literal or allegorical exegesis could be made to prefigure the Christ and the Christian message. That the books of the minor prophets do contain some Messianic passages is agreed to by both Jews and Christians. All except Obadiah and Nahum are quoted or echoed in the New Testament. These passages are significant background study for the New Testament student and attention will be called to them in the lessons on the several books.

7

These lessons, however, are built upon the assumption that the prophets first had a message relevant to the moral and religious situation of their own day. It is the duty of the expositor to try first to set forth that message. But of what value, other than to satisfy curiosity, can such a message be? While it is granted that times have changed and new gadgets have become abundant, it is denied that the basic issues of life are different today from those of the days of the prophets. Men still trust in material strength and delight in wealth and luxury while they forget God. There is nothing particularly new about lying, killing, stealing, and committing adultery. Oppression and injustice are rampant. Men still tend to heed the speaker who presents the pleasant message and assures them that their deeds are satisfactory. Men prefer to make amends by sacrifice rather than to do right. The prophets, properly interpreted, speak to these issues as though they were among us today, presenting their thoughts in unforgettable figures of speech. The prophets insist that God—rather than economics or politics—is the final arbiter of history. Their message will never be out of date.

Basic Principles for Understanding the Prophets

A. The prophet is a man who is moved by the Holy Spirit (2 Peter 1:20, 21).

B. The prophet cannot introduce strange religions (Deut. 13:1-5). Prophets did not introduce a new law. It was their function to call men back to the law given by Moses.

C. The true prophet is the man whose oracles come to pass (Deut. 18:20-22). The ability to know the future belongs to God alone. The prophet knows things to come only to the extent that God speaks through him.

D. Prophecy is conditional (Jer. 18:5-11). The question must be kept before you: Have the conditions of this threat or promise been met? Remember that the Lord did not destroy Nineveh despite Jonah's threat, for Nineveh repented. A threat may be delayed by repentance (cf. 1 Kings 21:29).

E. The prophets lived before and immediately after the

Assyrian and Babylonian exiles. Threats of destruction are fulfilled in these calamities. The return promised is the return from Babylon. Zechariah reminds the post-exilic people that the threats against their fathers are fulfilled (Zech. 1:5, 6).

F. Christ's first coming and the beginning of the church are important subjects of Old Testament prophecy (Rom. 1:2; Acts 3:24-26; 1 Peter 1:10-12).

G. God's final revelation is made in his Son (Heb. 1:1, 2). It is for this reason that when a New Testament writer says "This is that which was spoken by the prophet" it is to be considered as conclusive for that particular prophetic statement.

A General Preview of the Place of The Minor Prophets in the Prophetic Movement

A prophet is primarily a spokesman for another person (Exod. 4:10-16; 7:1). Through him God revealed his will in the Old Testament period (Heb. 1:1). He is sometimes also called a "seer" (1 Sam. 9:9), a "man of God" (1 Kings 13:1), or a "man of the spirit" (Hos. 9:7), but it is "prophet" (*nabi*) which is the more common term. *Nabi* occurs about 400 times as a noun in the Old Testament, and a verb from the same root occurs 110 times. This verb root, sometimes thought to be related to ecstatic behaviour, is now based on an analogy with Akkadian *nabu,* more widely thought to present the idea of "calling." It is still debated whether it is active or passive, that is, whether the prophet is "the called one" or the one who "calls out." Both elements form a part of the prophet's activity. He is called of God and he proclaims the will of God.

Prophecy is clearly distinguished in Scripture from magic, soothsaying, divining, augury, and other means so well known to middle eastern people by which they sought to know the will of the deity and the future. Nine different types of such activity are specifically prohibited the Israelite in Deuteronomy 18, while the prophet is a figure raised up by God as the watchman on the wall to warn his people (Ezek. 33).

Beginning with Abraham, numerous figures of the Old

Testament are called prophets. Moses is always looked up to
as the prophet *par excellence* (Deut. 18:15 ff.). Women like
Deborah (Judg. 4:4), Miriam (Exod. 15:20), and Huldah (2
Kings 22:14) enjoy this gift. However, after the time of
Samuel prophetic figures seem to become more numerous and
we meet Nathan (2 Sam. 7), Ahijah (1 Kings 11:29), Elijah
(1 Kings 17 ff.), Elisha (2 Kings 2 ff.), Micaiah ben Imlah (1
Kings 22), and others.

Efforts have been made to connect the appearance of
prophets with crises in Israel's history, and there may be
some validity to this effort. Samuel appears in the time of the
Philistine danger. Elijah is the opponent of Jezebel. Elisha is
active against the Arameans of Damascus; and Amos, Hosea,
Micah, and others arise when Assyria is about to swallow up
Israel. The early prophets, however, did not leave behind
them books that are collections of their oracles. It is not until
the eighth century B.C. that such collections are found. For
this reason it is common to distinguish between the early
prophets and the writing prophets though they are one and
all designated in Scripture by the same term—*nabi*. Prophecy
was thought by the rabbis to have come to an end following
the time of Malachi (1 Maccabees 4:46; 14:41; Josephus,
Apion I.8).

Prophets also existed among the neighbors of Israel. There
were the prophets of Baal (1 Kings 18:19) and of Asherah (1
Kings 18:19) and the prophets learned of in the excavations
of the city of Mari. There were prophets who, while claiming
to speak in the name of Jehovah, opposed the prophets like
Micaiah (1 Kings 22) or Jeremiah (Jer. 28). There were bands
of prophets and prophets that stand out as single individuals.
However, Biblical Hebrew has only the name *nabi* ("prophet")
for all of these figures.

The pantomime or symbolic action forms one means by
which the prophet conveys his message. A long list of examples can be collected from the prophets in general. Since
we do not have personal details about most of the minor
prophets, it cannot be known to what extent they engaged in

symbolic acts. The marriage of Hosea and the names of his children do fall in the category of symbolism.

The Name and the Arrangement of the Books

The designation for the minor prophets which is regularly used in early Jewish and Christian sources is "The Book of the Twelve" or "The Twelve Prophets" (Ecclesiasticus 49:10; Josephus, *Apion* I.8; Eusebius, *H.E.* 4.26.14). Augustine seems to have contributed the name "Minor Prophets" (*City of God* 18.29).

These books are not "minor" in the sense of being less important nor are they all later in date than the major prophets. A minor prophet may be equally important to a major one. The major and minor prophets overlap each other in date. The name seems to refer to length only. A "major" prophet, in general, is a longer book than is a "minor" prophet.

While these books were originally separate scrolls, and while we have no specific external information on the process of their assimilation into one collection, it would seem that length and date played a part. The Assyrian period prophets are placed first and the Persian period last. Within these periods the longer prophets come before the shorter ones. However, no theory is satisfactory to explain the position of every book. In the fourth century A.D. Greek manuscripts Codex Vaticanus and Alexandrinus the minor prophets precede the major prophets, but in the Latin version and other versions it is customary to place them after the major prophets. In this practice the current English Bible has followed the serial order and place order of the Hebrew Bible.

The Times of the Prophets

It is obvious that you could not understand the life of George Washington if you were not clear on whether he was a Revolutionary War or a Civil War figure. In like manner, you cannot understand the prophets until you make clear in your mind what period of Israel's history and with what international relations they deal. The prophets should be thought of as dealing with current events of their day.

Begin with the Bible itself. The prophets fit into Israel's history in the period covered by 2 Kings 14:23 to the end of that book together with the books of Ezra and Nehemiah. The more you know about this period of history, the better you can deal with the prophets.

There is also a great deal of material from archaeology that you should not overlook, which is relevant to the prophets. The minor prophets span three periods of history in which Israel and Judah are dominated by foreign nations: (1) The Assyrian Period: A. Parrot, *Nineveh and the Old Testament* (London: SCM Press, 1955) will help you on the details; (2) The Babylonian Period: A. Parrot, *Babylon and the Old Testament* (London: SCM Press, 1958) has the basic facts here; (3) The Persian Period: Charles Pfeiffer, *Exile and Return* (Grand Rapids: Baker Book House, 1962) should be read.

It is particularly significant to fix in mind the following events:

721 B.C.   The fall of Samaria to Assyria and the exile of the Northern Kingdom.

612 B.C.   The fall of Nineveh to the onslaught of Babylonians, Medes and Scythians.

606 B.C.   The battle of Carchemish by which Babylon became dominant in the Middle East.

597 B.C.   The fall of Jerusalem to Nebuchadnezzar and the exile of King Jehoiachin.

586 B.C.   The destruction of Jerusalem by Nebuchadnezzar.

539 B.C.   The beginning of the Persian Period.

536 B.C.   The decree of Cyrus permitting the return from exile and the reconstruction of the temple. The return led by Zerubbabel.

520 B.C.   The work of Haggai and Zechariah to stir up the people to resume work on the temple.

516 B.C.   The completion and dedication of the second temple.

457 B.C. The return led by Ezra.
445 B.C. Nehemiah rebuilds the walls of Jerusalem.

Classification of the Minor Prophets
by Historical Periods

Assyrian Period 8th-7th Cent. B.C.	Babylonian Period 7th Cent. B.C.	Persian Period or Post-Exilic Prophets 6th-5th Cent. B.C.
Jonah	Habakkuk	Haggai
Amos		Zechariah
Hosea		Malachi
Micah		
Zephaniah		
Nahum		

It is not certain at what date Joel and Obadiah prophesied; therefore they have not been included in the table. Drill yourself until you automatically associate each prophet with his proper period.

Only Jonah, Amos, and Hosea are primarily concerned with matters of relevance to the Northern Kingdom. In one sense Hosea is the only writing prophet who is a prophet of the Northern Kingdom. For Amos and Hosea, study the rapid exchange of kings following Jeroboam II. For the other prophets, study the reigns of Hezekiah, Manasseh, Josiah, Jehoiachim, Jehoiachin, and Zedekiah. Do not overlook the early stages of return from exile which furnish the setting for the Persian period prophets.

The Books of the Prophets

The books of the minor prophets show a wide range of literary types. Amos and Hosea contain a combination of stories about the prophet as well as collections of his oracles. Jonah, on the other hand, is largely taken up with the story of a prophet and has only a small part of its material made up of what the prophet preached. Nahum is entirely made up of oracles of the prophet. Zechariah has a large series of visions, while Malachi is made up of a series of arguments between the prophet and his hearers. Habakkuk raises questions with God, speaking to God rather than the reverse that is customary in the books. Haggai dates his oracles, while the dating of most of the other prophetic material is involved in considerable conjecture.

The books of the prophets tend to be rhythmical in form. Recent translations like the RSV attempt to reproduce this rhythm in poetic form. The student will find the prophets clearer if he makes use of such a translation because it makes use of recent discoveries related to vocabulary, because it expresses itself in modern English, and because it contains rhythmical structure.

New Materials on the Text

A chance discovery by a Bedouin goatherd in 1947 of a cave containing manuscripts touched off a search that has wrought considerable change in our knowledge of the text of the minor prophets. Since 1947 eleven caves near the north end of the Dead Sea have furnished manuscripts of biblical books much older than those previously known by approximately 1,000 years. Cave 1, the cave found by the goatherd, had a full text and commentary on Habakkuk 1-2 as well as fragments of Hosea and Micah. Cave 2 had scraps of Jonah. Cave 4 had parts of all the minor prophets except Obadiah, Habakkuk, and Haggai. There were also minor commentaries on Hosea and Nahum. From other caves in the area the remainder of the books are represented at least in fragments.

The Bedouin have also found a leather Greek scroll of the minor prophets dating from 50 B.C. to A.D. 50, which would be much older than the fourth century Greek manuscripts previously known, and, unlike those, would not be the work of a Christian scribe. This scroll now resides in the Palestine Archaeological Museum. The location where it was found has not been revealed.

Prior to these discoveries the oldest Hebrew manuscripts

for the minor prophets were from the tenth century A.D. The new manuscripts not only move us much nearer the time of the composition of the books, but also take us behind the period of Masoretic activity (A.D. 500-1000) at which time the currently used system of indicating vowels was developed. In addition we can see from the commentaries how the prophets were interpreted in the community that produced and stored the scrolls.

DISCUSSION

1. What is the basic task of a prophet?
2. What are some of the categories of prophets encountered in the Old Testament?
3. What are the basic differences between major and minor prophets?
4. During what periods of Israel's history were the prophets active?
5. From memory arrange the minor prophets according to the international crises in which they played a part.
6. Explain the plan of arrangement of books in the latter part of the Old Testament.
7. How is it to be explained that some predictions made by the prophets do not seem to have come to pass?
8. How do the books of the minor prophets differ from each other?
9. Of what value are the Dead Sea Scrolls for the study of the minor prophets?
10. Is the present age the subject of Old Testament prophecy?

Chapter II

THE PROPHET AMOS

The Prophet

Amos was a herdsman of an ugly type of sheep with fine wool called a *noked*. He lived in the village of Tekoa, which is twelve miles south of Jerusalem and six miles south of Bethlehem. Tekoa is a desolate region in the summer, too dry for the cultivation of grain, 2700 feet above sea level, which looks off into the abyss of the Dead Sea, eighteen miles away. Certain seasons out of the year Amos migrated either into the coastal plain or to the Jordan valley to tend sycamore trees which in Palestine produce a sort of fruit that must be pierced to ripen. He went through no other special training to prepare him for his task of being a prophet.

Amos dates his activity as being during the reigns of Uzziah (called Azariah in 2 Kings 15:1 ff.), king of Judah (783-742 B.C.), and Jeroboam II, king of Israel (786-746 B.C.), two years before the earthquake. We have no further definite information about this earthquake, except that it must have been of considerable magnitude, for four hundred years later people were still referring to it (Zech. 14:5); and Josephus (*Antiquities* 9.10.4) informs us—we know not how reliably—that it took place in connection with Uzziah's trespass reported in 2 Chronicles 26:18-21.

Amos prophesied in Bethel (7:10) and was denounced by Amaziah, the priest, and forbidden to preach further in Israel. Amos' reply was, "I was not a prophet and I was not a son of a prophet, but God called me to prophesy to Israel." Hebrew does not express the verb "to be" under certain circumstances, which leaves the translator with the problem of supplying a verb. It would seem that the past tense may be

16

supplied here, for Amos must describe the activity in which he is engaging as prophesying (7:15), which makes it difficult to conceive of his saying, "I am no prophet." Amos thinks of prophets as being raised up by the Lord (2:11) who reveals his secrets to his prophets (3:7, 8). Whether Amos prophesied elsewhere other than Bethel as some have argued is uncertain. J. Morgenstern argued that there was only one speech on one occasion. The prophet does not enlighten us concerning what happened to him after his encounter with Amaziah.

The Call of the Prophet

Several of the prophets relate specifically the circumstances that set them on their prophetic career. Though Amos is not specific concerning when he saw the five visions of chapters 7-9, perhaps it will do the prophet no violence to consider these as his call.

a. The locusts (7:1-3). Locusts in Palestine were uncontrollable and considered "an act of God." Amos saw in them the threat of God's punishment and by pleading caused the Lord to relent.

b. The great fire devouring the land (7:4-6). Again the prophet pleads and the Lord relents.

c. The plumb line (7:7-9). The Lord announces judgment against his people that involves the doom of the house of Jeroboam. Amos does not plead further.

d. The basket of summer fruit (8:1, 2). Prophets frequently convey their message by puns not intended to be humorous. From the similarity of summer (*qayits*) and end (*qets*) the Lord teaches Amos that the end is at hand. "The end has come upon my people Israel" (8:2).

e. Amos sees the Lord standing by the altar and giving the command to smite the capitals and let none escape (9:1).

The Structure of the Book

It is not uncommon for a prophetic book to have three elements: (a) oracles against nations, (b) oracles of doom for

Israel, and (c) oracles of hope. The book of Amos has each of these elements.

The first two chapters of Amos are taken up with oracles against the neighbors of Israel. A common pattern is followed in which the sins are specified and the punishment is announced. This pattern is repeated seven times and then is turned on Israel.

Chapters 3, 4, and 5 each begin with "Hear this word" followed by denunciation of the sins of Israel with appropriate comments drawn from God's past dealings with Israel.

Chapters 7, 8, and 9 begin with "The Lord showed me" or "I saw" and the visions of Amos, interspersed with further denunciation of sins, are given.

Finally, the book closes with oracles of hope (9:11-15).

The Neighbors of Israel

God will punish the neighbors of Israel for their abundant (three or four) transgressions: (1) Damascus has, in the course of its border exchanges with Israel, threshed Gilead with threshing instruments of iron. The punishment will be that the strength of the various districts about Damascus will be broken and the Syrians will be exiled to Kir from whence they came (Amos 9:7). (2) The people of Gaza have delivered an unnamed population into slavery to Edom. Consequently, the Philistine cities will be destroyed. Of the Philistine cities, Gath is unmentioned by Amos. (3) The same crime as that of Philistia is laid at the feet of Tyre. She further has not remembered the covenant of brotherhood. Tyre shall be destroyed. (4) Edom has pursued his brother with the sword. The perpetual enmity between Israel and Edom seems to be here reflected. (5) The Ammonites have ripped up pregnant women of Gilead in order to enlarge their border. Exile awaits them. (6) Moab has desecrated the bones of the King of Edom. (7) Judah has rejected the law of God and not kept his statutes. Punishment also awaits her.

The significant thing about this series, which in general denounces atrocities of war, is that Amos announces that God

is concerned with sin wherever it occurs. God is not merely a
god of the hills limited in power and dominion to his own
people. He is the international God of justice punishing sin
wherever it occurs, calling the neighbors who do not worship
him into account.

The Sins of Israel

Having gained the attention of the audience by denouncing
the behaviour of the neighbors, Amos in scathing terms denounces Israel. For a trifle they have forced the righteous into
slavery: "sold the righteous for silver and the needy for a
pair of shoes" (2:6, 7). They have oppressed the poor (5:7,
11). Bribes are accepted (5:12). They have traded with dis-
honest scales and measures (8:5, 6). In the face of these
Amos calls for justice: "Let justice roll down as waters and
righteousness as a mighty stream" (5:24). They must hate
evil and love good (5:15).

The father and his son have relations with the same maiden
(2:7). They have shut the mouths of the prophets who might
have denounced them (2:12; 5:10).

A general materialism has settled upon them and holds all
in its grip. Women, whose insatiable desire for finery drives
their husbands to oppression, stretched out on their couches
of ivory, call each to her husband, "Mix us another drink"
(4:1). The people have their summer houses and winter
houses (3:15) and their beds of ivory (6:4). At ease in Zion,
the people eat the finest food, anoint themselves with fine oil,
and invent instruments of music like David for their enter-
tainment, but do not concern themselves with the approaching ruin of their country (Chap. 6).

Neglect of religious forms by the people was not a problem Amos faced. On the contrary, there seems to have been
considerable zeal for festivals and offerings (4:4, 5). A false
confidence in their own righteousness said, "God is with us"
(5:14) and "No evil will befall us" (9:10).

Past warnings of the Lord, numerous as they have been,
have gone unheeded. Prophets and Nazarites have been

rejected (2:11, 12). Famine, drought, blight, pestilence, battle, and earthquake have brought no repentance. Israel is a brand plucked from burning (4:7-11; cf. Zech 3:2). John Wesley narrowly escaped a fire as a child and often described himself with this phrase. God must use sterner measures. Israel must prepare to face God (4:12).

The Lion Roars

In the face of such sins, Amos can only sing the funeral song of Israel (5:1, 2). In the regular funeral meter he laments that Israel is fallen to rise no more. For the first time in Hebrew literature the whole nation is styled "virgin." The specific enemy is not mentioned, but the lion (perhaps of Assyria, that is, the Lord roars through the Assyrian Lion) is roaring (1:2). A nation is to oppress them (6:14); Israel will go into exile beyond Damascus (5:27). Amaziah will die in an alien land while his wife will be a harlot (7:17). Amos is the first of the prophets to threaten the Northern Kingdom with exile. The Day of the Lord must be faced (5:18). It is a doom as inevitable as though facing a lion, bear, and serpent in one day, and though at first escaping, finally being bitten by the serpent. It is a pitiable trifle that will escape. The shepherd rescued from the lion or bear the remains of the lamb as evidence to attest his innocence of the charge of abusing the flock (Exod. 22:13). Two legs and a piece of an ear of a lamb are not much, but so the witness to Israel would be left (Amos 3:12).

Amos' threats were not long delayed in coming. In 735 Ahaz of Judah appealed to Tiglath Pileser III to aid him in his struggle against Damascus and Israel (Pekah and Rezin: Isa. 7). By 733 Tiglath Pileser overran and deported the northern and eastern portions of Israel (2 Kings 15:29). His campaigns are also attested in his own inscriptions. In 722, less than a generation after Amos, Samaria was besieged by Shalmaneser V and fell. Sargon II, successor to Shalmaneser, claims that he exiled 27,290 Israelites from Samaria. The Lion had roared and taken prey. Israel was no more.

Key Concepts

The Day of the Lord. Amos presents for the first time the concept of "The Day of the Lord" (5:18). It is obvious that he has taken up a popular expression that to the people expressed hope. It is the day on which they would be victorious. Amos inverts the phrase to a concept of doom—a day of darkness and not of light. We do not know how the idea arose. It is a day, not at the end of history, but within the framework of history when the fate of a nation is realized. This concept, which reappears in later prophets, should be studied diligently.

Strongholds that are not strong. Amos vigorously attacked the false confidence of the people:

a. God is our God and we are his people. This Amos does not deny, but insists that they are really no more to God than the Ethiopians (9:7). The very fact that they are God's people demands their punishment. "You only have I known of the people of the earth and therefore I must visit your sins upon you" (3:2). Privilege involves responsibility.

b. God brought Israel out of Egypt (2:10). The implication is that God could not now abandon Israel in midstream. Amos points out that God is also responsible for other migrations (9:7, 8). There is no basis for complacency here.

c. We worship God regularly. In bitter irony the prophet suggests that they step up the tempo of worship (4:4, 5). At the same time he makes clear that God hates and despises their worship (Amos 5:21). God demands right rather than rites (5:23, 24).

The Dilapidated Tent of David

The third section of the book of Amos speaks of a day when reaping will turn to sowing. It envisions a fertile and prosperous land and a people restored to that land (9:13-15). Need it be pointed out that Zerubbabel led back exiles and reestablished them in the land in the sixth century B.C.?

The broken down tent of David (the royal house, cf. 2 Sam. 7) will again be set up (Amos 9:11, 12).

Amos and the New Testament

Two sections of Amos are appealed to in the New Testament: Stephen (Acts 7:42, 43) appeals to Amos 5:25-27 to establish that Israel was disloyal already in the wilderness. Stephen uses "beyond Babylon" to describe the threat of exile instead of "beyond Damascus" which is in the text of Amos to correspond to known facts of the exile.

James (Acts 15) found the promise of the restored tent of David (Amos 9:11, 12) a basis upon which to justify the Gentile mission. The point made by James is that the tabernacle has been rebuilt; hence the Gentiles may seek the Lord. It is interesting to notice that the new covenant sect from the Dead Sea area (*Cairo Damascus Document* 7:11 ff.) also appealed to each of these two passages to justify their existence.

DISCUSSION

1. Out of the book of Amos, what passages do you find more appealing than others?
2. What has Amos to teach us about the relationship of privilege and responsibility?
3. Are there parallels to be seen between the position occupied by Israel and the position occupied by the church?
4. In what way were the doctrines of Amos concerning God novel for his day?
5. How similar are the sins of Amos' day to sins of our own day?
6. What is Amos' alternative to destruction? Is there such an alternative in the book?
7. What did "The Day of the Lord" mean to the people of Amos' day? What did it mean to the prophet?
8. Are there unfulfilled prophecies in the book of Amos?
9. Is the God of Amos a God of justice or of mercy? What is your evidence?

10. What evidence have we that prophets played a role in political uprisings?

READINGS ON AMOS

In addition to the general treatments of the minor prophets, the student may find that the following books on Amos will give him additional information.

Cripps, Richard S., *A Critical and Exegetical Commentary on the Book of Amos* (London: SPCK, 1929).

Edgehill, E. A., *The Book of Amos* (London: Methuen and Co., 1914).

Honeycutt, Roy Lee, *Amos and His Message* (Nashville: Broadman Press, 1963).

Kapelrud, A. S., *Central Ideas in Amos* (Oslo: Oslo University Press, 1961).

Watts, John D. W., *Vision and Prophecy in Amos* (Leiden: E. J. Brill, 1958).

Chapter III

THE PROPHET HOSEA

Introduction

The name "Hosea" means "God is salvation." The prophet is the son of Beeri, but we know nothing else of Beeri. Hosea has the distinction of being the only writing prophet of the Northern Kingdom. (Amos was from the south and preached to the north; Jonah, though from Galilee, preached to Nineveh.) In the book the Northern Kingdom is usually called Ephraim from its largest tribe. All of Hosea's imagery comes from the north. The other details of his personal life are wrought into the fabric of his book so that it is better to study them as a part of the book.

Though the rabbis contended that Hosea was the first of the prophets (a notion based upon a fallacious interpretation resulting from stress on "first" in Hosea 1:2: "When the Lord first spoke to Hosea"), Hosea really seems to have prophesied in the years following 746 B.C., slightly after the time of Amos.

The Assyrian aggression got under way anew with the accession of Tiglath Pileser III in 745 B.C. and the handwriting was on the wall for Israel. While Amos did not name the enemy who threatened, Hosea is specific that it is Assyria (7:11; 11:5; 11; 12:1; 14:3). The Indian summer period of the reign of Jeroboam II gave way to the instability of the final days as kings were cut off "like a chip [foam: KJV] on water" (Hos. 10:7). Kings were given in anger and taken away in wrath (Hos. 13:11), blood touched blood (Hos. 4:2). In 2 Kings 15:8-17:41 is a summary of this tragic period of 25 years in which six kings reigned: Zechariah, Shallum, Menahem, Pekahiah, Pekah, and Hoshea. Four of these were

murdered in office by their successors and one was captured
in battle. Only one (Menahem) was succeeded on the throne
by his son. Terms of office were as brief as one month. In one
short year Zechariah, Shallum, and Menahem succeeded each
other.

The dismemberment of the Northern Kingdom got under
way in 735 when Tiglath Pileser III of Assyria took Gilead and
carried off the people of Naphtali. Shortly afterward Hoshea
conspired with So, king of Egypt, against Assyria. Hoshea
was arrested by Shalmaneser V and the city of Samaria was
besieged three years until its capitulation. Sargon claims to
have carried off 27,290 people in 721 B.C. and foreigners
were settled in Samaria in their place (2 Kings 17:24). The
exile had set in; Israel was no more. The student is urged to
make use of A. Parrot, *Nineveh and the Old Testament* (London: SCM Press, 1953, 96 pp.), in surveying the background
of this period.

The Structure of the Book

The book of Hosea is one of the most difficult of the minor
prophets. The text is in a poor condition. There seems to be
no outline that can be reconstructed. However, the book may
be divided into two sections. Chapters 1-3 present the marriage of Hosea and his family. Chapter 1 tells of his marriage
to Gomer and of her children with the story told in the third
person. Chapter 2 is an allegorization of the relationship to
Gomer to make the marriage symbolize the Lord's relationship
to Israel. Chapter 3 tells of Hosea's marriage in the first person.

The second portion of the book of Hosea, Chapters 4-14,
presents the prophet's attack upon Israel's involvement in the
Canaanite cult.

The Family of the Prophet

Hosea's life is made to be a walking lesson of the message
he had to preach. He is commanded by the Lord to marry a

woman of harlotry and beget children of harlotry. He marries
Gomer, daughter of Diblaim (1:2, 3).

To this family there were born three children, each of whom
is given a name that is a part of the prophet's preaching. The
first, a son, is called Jezreel, as a threat to the reigning house,
which was soon to end. It was at Jezreel that Jehu established
his dynasty (2 Kings 9:16). Jezreel seems to be punned on
here in a possible meaning "God scatters." It is to be ob-
served, however, that Jezreel can also mean "God sows";
therefore, a two-fold play on the boy's name, the second of
which plays is a hopeful element (Hos. 1:11; 2:22, 23), is
encountered in the book.

The second child, a daughter named "not pitied," is a
threat that God will not pity and forgive the house of Israel.
The third is a son called "not my people." When it is remembered that the formula of the covenant is "I will be your
God and you shall be my people" (Lev. 26:12), the threat
contained in this child's name obviously is that of the break-
ing of the relationship. Since the text does not say "bore *him*
a son" or "bore *him* a daughter" (ch. 1:3; cf. vss. 6, 8) in
connection with these last two children, many students have
felt that the prophet knew that they were not really his
children.

One of the most perplexing questions of the book is the
question of the relationship of the woman of Chapter 3 to
that of Chapter 1. Gomer could have died meanwhile; plural
marriage was not unknown in ancient Israel and of course is
possible here. Some have seen the woman of Chapter 3 to be
Gomer who is now bought back, half in money and half in
produce, to the equal of the price of a slave. The interpretation is dependent upon what meaning is assigned to Chapter
3:1—whether it is "go again love" or "go on loving." Both are
possible translations. There is to be a period of isolation that
may be compared with the end of the monarchy.

Equally perplexing is the question of the original character
of Gomer. Revolting at the idea of God's commanding a man
to do something repulsive, Ibn Ezra and others have attempted to allegorize the whole, but such action on the

prophet's part is somewhat against human nature. This is not the type of story one tells on his wife if there is not some fact in it, nor does the meaning of the name "Gomer" lend itself easily to an allegory. Others have attempted to establish that Gomer, though faithful at first, was a woman of a weak character who then developed into open moral laxity. As one later in life might say of his mate, "I married a drunkard," meaning that she became a drunkard in time, so Gomer was potentially a harlot. This, of course, makes a nice parallel to the relationship between God and Israel. Israel was once loyal to God. Be the solution what it may, the Lord taught Hosea by means of his own broken down marriage that God's attitude to Israel was not essentially different from that of Hosea to Gomer. God loved Israel.

In Hosea's book Israel is both "wife" and "son." In Gomer we have the picture of the prodigal wife. But in presenting the same concept of the nature of God, Hosea also anticipates the Prodigal Son. Israel is God's son who has been brought out of Egypt (cf. Exod. 4:22 f.). What a heart-rending thought is presented as God took Israel, the child, by hand and taught him to walk (Hos. 11:1-9), but Israel, now grown up, has rebelled! How could God abandon the prodigal son? He must forgive. Thus Hosea knows the idea of the Fatherhood of God. He is both the offended father and the offended husband.

The Worship of Baal

The book of Hosea can only be understood against the background of Canaanite religion and Israel's involvement in it. When Israel came into Palestine she came into a land already inhabited for more than a thousand years. She learned farming from the peoples she did not drive out. But Canaanite farming was integrally connected with religious customs that Israel adopted as the Pilgrims learned from the Indians to put two fish on each side of a grain of corn. Subtly the religion crept in on them.

We have at our disposal three major sources for information

on Canaanite religion. One is Hosea, a second is the historian
Eusebius, but more recently the discoveries at Ras Shamra in
Syria have brilliantly enlightened us (see Charles Pfeiffer,
Ras Shamra and the Bible [Grand Rapids: Baker Book House,
1962], 73 pp.).

El, Baal, and Dagon were leading deities in the Canaanite
pantheon, but these had their female counterparts in Asherah,
Astarte, and Anath. Worship centered in the high place which
was an open air shrine with a wooden object to represent the
female divinity and a stone object for the male. Priests and
sacred persons (male and female) were in attendance. Sacrifices and festivals were regular features. The major object
of the rites was to obtain fertility for man, animal and field.
Ritual fornication and bestiality were engaged in.

Some Key Concepts in Hosea

1. *Knowledge of God.* The proper relationship of men to
God is to know the Lord. Whereas some parts of Scripture
emphasize the "fear of God," Hosea emphasizes knowledge.
The word *yada'* in Hebrew is used to describe a man's relation to his wife (Gen. 4:1)—the most intimate experience
that is humanly possible. With Hosea, to know God is no
mere intellectual matter, but is rather an intimate relationship
that comes by living with and for him and must be persistently
pursued (6:3). Without it there is killing, stealing, and false
swearing (4:1, 2). The people are destroyed for lack of
knowledge (4:6; 13:4; John 17:3). It is knowledge of God
and mercy that God demands more than sacrifice (Hos. 6:6).

2. *Hesed.* Hesed was translated "loving kindness" by
Coverdale (A.D. 1535) and those who came after him, but
also sometimes is "mercy." The term occurs six times in Hosea
and is a related idea both to grace and loyalty (2:19; 4:1;
6:6; 10:12; 12:6). This word implying covenant loyalty, which
does not occur in Amos, will merit a lot of study.

3. *Spiritual Adultery.* Hosea's relationship to Gomer and
what it teaches lays the basis for thinking of disloyalty to
God as "spiritual adultery" (4:15-18; 5:4; 9:1). Hosea uses

the term whoredom sixteen times. Israel's marriage relationship goes back to a betrothal period in the wilderness, but in
Canaan she had gone after her lovers, the Baals. Before she
can return to her husband, she must be taken back to the
wilderness (2:14).

Israel's Sins

1. Resorting to the high places where they loved to offer
sacrifice (8:13): From Baal they sought grain, wine, and
oil (2:5-7, 13; 4:10-13; 9:10; 10:1, 2; 13:1, 2). The deepness
of this penetration can be seen in names compounded with
Baal such as Ishbaal, Baaljada, Meribbaal, etc. Hosea threatens that the names of Baal will be taken from the mouth (2:16,
17). A reaction against Baal can be seen as the name Ishbaal
becomes Ishbosheth (2 Sam. 2:8; cf. 1 Chron. 8:33).

2. Traffic with the sacred women at the local shrines which
profaned God's name (4:14; cf. Deut. 23:17; 1 Kings 14:24;
15:12).

3. Open idolatry (13:2): They revered the calf images of
Samaria (8:5; 10:5 f.). Hosea is the first of the writing prophets to attack the bull cult (13:2), which had also been attacked by the unnamed prophet (1 Kings 13).

4. International intrigue: Like a silly dove that will
eventually be caught, Israel seeks first Assyria and next Egypt
(5:13; 7:8-11). She seeks international trade which carried
with it temptations to adopt international culture (12:1-7).

5. Israel's trust in material armaments instead of in the
Lord (10:13).

The Alternative to Destruction

Israel has sown the wind and reaps the whirlwind (8:7).
She has plowed iniquity and reaped injustice (10:13). It is
time to seek the Lord—time to break up fallow ground (10:
12). It is well to keep in mind that: (1) One reaps what he
sows (Gal. 6:7). (2) There is ordinarily an increase in reap-

ing over the sowing. (3) The reaping is proportional to sowing (2 Cor. 9:6). (4) While weeds grow with less care than wheat, wheat is a more profitable crop.

Chapter 6 is a call to repentance. Chapter 14 is another call to repentance in which there is an appeal to forsake idols and return to the Lord. The Lord promises forgiveness, healing, and blessings. Hosea is the prophet of God's love.

The Messianic Hope

Hosea 3:5 looks for a time when Israel will seek the Lord and David their king. In the latter days they will come in fear to the Lord and his goodness.

Hosea in the New Testament

1. "Not my people" (Rom. 9:25, 26; 1 Peter 2:10; cf. Hos. 2:23; 1:10). The New Testament writers reveal to us that those who were not God's people but who become his people are the Gentiles.

2. "I desire mercy and not sacrifice" (Hos. 6:6; Matt. 9: 13; 12:7; cf. Mark 12:33). With this statement Jesus rebuked those who found fault because he had mercy on sinners and because his disciples ate grain on the Sabbath.

3. "Out of Egypt have I called my son" (Hos. 11:1; cf. Exod. 4:22 f.; Matt. 2:15). The application of this passage from Hosea—which in its context clearly refers to the exodus experience of Israel—to the experience of Jesus makes it quite clear that Matthew understands the word "fulfill" to include typical fulfillment.

4. The wording of Hosea is adapted to describe New Testament thoughts. (a) The terrors of the end of time when people call upon the hills to fall on them (Hos. 10:8; Luke 23:30; Rev. 6:16). (b) "Death, where is thy victory?" (Hos. 13:14; 1 Cor. 15:55). (c) Some have thought the idea of the resurrection on the third day (cf. 1 Cor. 15:4) is an interpretation of Hosea 6:1-2.

DISCUSSION

1. What part did a prophet's personal life play in his impact upon his society? Give specific examples.
2. What were the political conditions during the ministry of Hosea?
3. What are the chief reasons for assuming that Hosea's marriage is to be literally understood?
4. What was the appeal of the Baal worship to Israel?
5. What material in the Old Testament teaches the Fatherhood of God?
6. What is it to know the Lord?
7. What are various ways in which an Old Testament prophecy may be fulfilled?
8. Is the doom that Hosea threatens an inevitable one?
9. What influence on New Testament thought has Hosea's figure of adultery?
10. What lessons from Hosea do you find most applicable to the modern man?

BIBLIOGRAPHY

N. Snaith, *Mercy and Sacrifice* (London: SCM, 1953).

H. W. Robinson, *The Cross of Hosea* (Philadelphia: Westminster Press, 1959).

H. W. Robinson, *Two Hebrew Prophets* (London: Lutterworth Press, 1948).

Chapter IV

THE PROPHET MICAH

The Life and Times of the Prophet

The sixth in the biblical sequence of the minor prophets is Micah. Micah (a shortened form of Micaiah, cf. 1 Kings 22), which name means "Who is like Yahweh?" lived at Moresheth-Gath on the main road to the Maritime plain and Egypt in the Shephelah (the foothill country) off about 25 miles southwest of Jerusalem. The city, which lies at the edge of good farming country, is not elsewhere mentioned in Scripture.

Micah's ministry is dated by the reigns of Jothan, Ahaz, and Hezekiah, which gives a possible minimum span of 20 years and a maximum of 55. He is a prophet of the Southern Kingdom. One should study 2 Kings 15:32—20:21 and 2 Chron. 27:1—32:33 as a preparation for the study of this prophet. At this same period—the latter part of the eighth century B.C. —over in Jerusalem his contemporary Isaiah was prophesying. Perhaps slightly earlier in Israel, Hosea was active.

These years of the eighth century were earthshaking in their significance. The year 735 B.C. saw the Syro-Ephraimitic war as Pekah and Rezin threatened to depose Ahaz for his refusal to join them in a revolt against Assyria. They saw the Assyrian machine of aggression dismember Damascus and Israel in stages that led to the downfall of Samaria and to the exile of the northern tribes in 721 B.C. Ahaz maintained his state at the price of paying heavy tribute to Assyria, but in 711 B.C. the Philistine states were in a state of revolt which Sargon ruthlessly put down (Isa. 20). Sargon erected a victory stele at Ashdod, fragments of which have recently been recovered, as well as leaving behind in his palace at Khorsabad records of his victories in Palestine.

All of the dangers came to a climax in 701 B.C. when Hezekiah raised a revolt that brought Sennacherib west to demand his tribute and the surrender of Jerusalem. Siege was laid to Lachish which is near Moresheth-Gath. The city fell. Sennacherib left to posterity a large picture, today to be seen in the British Museum, which depicts his siege of Lachish. He boasts that he took 46 of Hezekiah's walled cities and shut the king up like a bird in a cage in his city, Jerusalem. The fact that Jerusalem was spared at the last moment does not affect the case that Micah's territory was devastated.

Micah, unlike Amos and Hosea, has left us no account of his call to prophesy or of other personal experiences. We know practically nothing of him as a person, but he was a man of the Spirit ready to prophesy (3:8).

The Book

The book of Micah does not lend itself to precise subject matter divisions. Chapters 1, 3, and 6 begin with "Hear ye" and each division ends with a promise.

Others have seen the book as most naturally falling into three sections: Chapters 1-3; Chapters 4-5; and Chapters 6-7.

The Sins of Judah

Micah, unlike his contemporary Isaiah, is a man of the country. His main concern is not international politics—the intrigues with Assyria and Egypt—nor does he chiefly exercise himself to be the advisor of kings, nor in the affairs of the court. The sins of immorality and sensuality characteristic of urban life receive little attention. His burden is the lot of the small farmer in the area of Moresheth-Gath, the oppressions he suffered, and the impact of the Assyrian invasion upon him. Micah deals with social morality and religious duty in a way that is distinctive to him.

1. Micah laments the disappearance of the righteous man
(7:2), reminding us of Abraham's plea for Sodom (Gen.
18:23 ff.), of Jeremiah's search in Jerusalem for a man doing
justice (Jer. 5:1), or of Diogenes and his lantern looking in
Athens for the honest man.

2. Micah has a quartet of evil doers. First there are the
avaricious land-grabbers who lay awake at night (2:1) to
figure out schemes to force the poor man off the land that
they might build such large estates (2:2) that they could not
see their nearest neighbor (Isa. 5:8). We can only recall
the fate of Naboth and his vineyard in the days of Ahab (1
Kings 21:4; cf. Mic. 6:16). Women and children were driven
out of house and home (2:9). The only consideration of the
powerful was: "I can get away with it. Why not do it?" No
one was to be trusted. A man might well be victimized by his
own relatives (7:5-7).

It must be remembered that Micah's society was not an
industrial one where the displaced man could get on at the
factory. The ideal was every man under his vine and every
man under his fig tree and no one to make them afraid (4:4).
The law of Moses forbade the selling of land perpetually and
the jubilee brought the land back to its traditional family
(Lev. 25:10, 23). Micah laments the scant measure (6:10,
11; cf. Deut. 25:13-16). There were problems of juvenile
delinquency (7:6). Such materialists were willing to listen
to preaching of wine and strong drink (2:11) but Micah was
an unwanted prophet. They refused to listen to the possibility
of disaster (2:6).

Second, there were the rulers who hated good and loved
evil (3:1-4), who instead of providing justice for the oppressed poor were open to bribes to decide cases in favor
of the biggest dollar (7:3) while closing their eyes at what
was going on (3:1). Micah compares them to butchers or
cannibals or to wild beasts (3:1-3). They think, he charges,
that Zion can be built with blood (3:10).

Third is the false prophet who divined for money (3:11).
The blessings of religion were given to the whole transaction.
Pay the prophet and he answers you that what you want to

do is right; neglect him and he declares war on you (3:5). It is to Micah that we owe some of our clearest material on the false prophet.

The fourth in the quartet is the priest who taught for hire (3:11) all the while thinking that the Lord was in their midst: "The Lord is with us, no evil shall befall us" (3:11).

3. Micah is not unaware of idolatry (5:12-15; cf. 3:7).

4. He faced a people who thought that because they were God's people their security would not be destroyed (3:11) and that God's favor could be bought with sacrifice (6:5-7).

The Threats of the Prophet

Micah is a prophet of judgment. The Lord comes from his place to execute it (1:3 ff.).

1. Samaria is to be overthrown (1:6, 7).

2. They had not heard the cry for mercy; God will not hear their cry (3:1-4).

3. Micah threatens the people with the failure of prophecy. They had not heeded the prophets that warned. In time of need the false prophet would be confounded and as much in the dark as if there had been an eclipse. There would be no guidance (3:6).

4. Micah is the first prophet specifically to threaten Judah with destruction of Jerusalem and its temple: "Zion shall be plowed like a field" (3:12). We learn from Jeremiah 26:18 that this threat brought repentance on the part of Hezekiah. The episode, however, is not alluded to in the historical books of the Old Testament so that we cannot know whether or not it lies back of the reforms of Hezekiah. It did save Jeremiah's life 100 years later when Jeremiah had also threatened the destruction of the temple. It is interesting to notice that men still remembered the words of the earlier prophet. This is one of the few cross references from one prophet to another in Scripture.

5. In the longest series of sustained puns in the Old Testament, Micah describes the advance of the Assyrian army through his section of country (1:10-16). Efforts to render

these into English may be seen in the translations of Moffat and Phillips: "Gad not Gath," etc. The invasion proceeds logically from the Philistine plain toward the north. We see one town after another become a victim. Saladin, Richard, and Allenby have attempted to reach Jerusalem by this route as did Sennacherib. This passage should be compared with Isaiah 10:28-34 where an advance from the north is presented.

6. The punishment will fit the crime. The land they have taken from the poor will be taken from them. Exile stares them in the face (1:16); they will go to Babylon (4:10). The people must be driven out as the Canaanites before them were driven out (2:10; cf. Deut. 9:5; 12:9); the land cannot tolerate a wicked population (Lev. 18:25).

True Religion According to Micah

In an unforgettable passage (6:1-8), Micah presents a court scene. There is the call to court with the hills of Palestine as the judges. God is the complainant and Israel is the defendant. How has God failed in his great acts of the past? The only possible answer is that he has not. His failure is not the cause of Israel's disloyalty.

Israel complains in self-defense that God's demands are unknowable. Rhetorical questions expecting a negative answer propose that God wants a multitude of offerings of calves or rams; or that God wants rivers of oil, or even the sacrifice of the first child (cf. Lev. 18:21; 2 Kings 16:3; and remember that Ahaz, Micah's contemporary, offered a son).

The prophet answers that in reality God's demands are three: justice, kindness, and walking humbly with God. T. H. Sutcliffe, *The Prophetic Road to God*, page 94, suggests that these are three elements stressed by Amos (Amos 5:24), Hosea (Hosea 6:6), and Isaiah (Isa. 16:5) respectively. This statement of Micah is universally recognized as one of the greatest passages of the Old Testament, stressing that worship and morality cannot be divorced from each other. They are two sides of the same coin.

Micah and the Future

1. *The Remnant.* Despite his severe threats, Micah is not a prophet devoid of hope. He envisons a remnant that will survive the calamity (2:12; 5:7, 8). This doctrine is greatly elaborated by his contemporary Isaiah.

2. *The New Exodus.* Micah envisions a return comparable to the exodus. God, at its head, leads the way as a ram opens the way for a flock (Exod. 13:21; cf. Mic. 2:12, 13). Micah speaks of marvels comparable to those of the exodus (7:14-17).

3. *The Law will go forth from Zion* (4:1 ff.). Micah and Isaiah (Isa. 2:2 ff.) in similar words describe this phenomenon, though each has his distinctive elements. We have no means of knowing which used it first. This is a passage not specifically appealed to in the New Testament, but which was understood by the early church fathers to refer to the Christian age (Justin Martyr, *Dial.* 110; Irenaeus, *Adv. Haer.* 4.34.4).

4. *The Messiah will be born in Bethlehem, the birthplace of David* (5:2; cf. 1 Sam. 17:12). Though 2 Samuel 7 connects the Messiah with the Davidic house, Micah is the first to point to his city. It is this passage that guided the wise men (Matt. 2:6).

5. *Mercy after Judgment* (7:18-20). The fundamental character of God is his mercy. Micah declares that the Lord is his light (7:8-10).

Micah in the New Testament

1. The Messiah from Bethlehem (5:2 f.; Matt. 2:6; John 7:42).

2. A man's enemies are those of his own household (7:6). Jesus found here words to describe the disturbance of society which his work made (Matt. 10:36; Luke 12:53).

3. The universalism of Micah's vision of peace (4:1-3) shows a kindred thought to Mark 11:17: "My house is a house of prayer for all people."

DISCUSSION

1. Contrast the conditions faced by Amos and those faced by Micah.
2. What motives made a man to be a false prophet?
3. What is the task of the true prophet as seen by Micah?
4. What brief summaries of man's duty other than that recorded by Micah are to be found in Scripture?
5. What are some of the high points in the development of the Messianic hope?
6. What moral and religious relevance has Micah's preaching to our day?
7. What are the implications of God's acts of the past as they are seen by Micah?
8. When were Micah's threats brought to fulfillment?
9. What are the significant items in Micah's vision of peace?
10. Is Micah opposed to worship by sacrifice?

Chapter V

THE PROPHET JONAH

Introduction

The book of Jonah—the fifth in sequence—is unique in the minor prophets in many ways. It is chiefly a book about a prophet instead of being a collection of oracles of the prophet. Only eight words are needed to report Jonah's preaching (Chap. 3:4). The book is the only latter prophet cast in narrative form, though there are some narrative sections in others, and the former prophets in the Hebrew Bible (Joshua —Kings) are narrative. Jonah is the only minor prophet in whose career the miraculous plays a prominent role, the only one whose major activity is on foreign soil, and the only one who preaches exclusively to a foreign people. Jonah is the only Old Testament character represented as taking a trip on the Mediterranean. Jonah is also the only minor prophet mentioned by Jesus and is the only Old Testament character likened by the Lord to himself (Matt. 12:38-41; 16:4; Luke 11:29-32). The book stresses universalism more than any other minor prophet. In the synagogue it is a part of the liturgy for the day of atonement.

Jonah, son of Amittai, is said to have preached in the Northern Kingdom in the days of Jeroboam II (2 Kings 14:25) and predicted victories over Syria. This episode, however, forms no part of the prophet's book. Jeroboam's reign was a time in which Israel extended her borders farther than at any period following the days of Solomon. It was a time of ease and prosperity, but at the same time on the horizon was Assyria who would eventually swallow up Israel. Already before this time Ahab and his allies had fought Shalmaneser III at Karkar and Jehu had paid tribute, which latter episode is depicted on the black obelisk left behind by Shalmaneser.

Jonah was from Gath-hepher, which is a few miles north of Nazareth. He is thereby a prophet from Galilee. Nineveh is 500 miles east of Palestine, as any map will reveal; therefore Jonah was fleeing the opposite direction as he attempted to go to Tarshish. It is thought by many that Tarshish is Tartessus in Spain, about 2,000 miles west of Palestine, and one of the most western points of call of the Phoenician trade. Jonah embarked from Joppa (modern Yafo), 50 miles from Gath-hepher, whose harbor, though small and unsafe, is the only one on the Palestinian coast below Mt. Carmel.

The Miracles

So much has been made of the "fish story" that one is tempted to forget all else about the book of Jonah. The facts are that the book is a book of numerous miracles—at least four—in which stress is great upon the fact that each event comes about as the direct act of God. One is not actually more natural than the other. These miracles are (1) the storm, (2) the calm, (3) the fish, and (4) the gourd, in all of which the power of God is displayed.

·Nevertheless, it is not out of place to take a look at the fish, which in Hebrew is *dag gadol* and is referred to only in three (1:17; 2:1, 10) out of the 48 verses of the book. *Dag* may be a fish of any species, including the whale (cf. Gen. 9:2; Num. 11:22; Neh. 13:16). In the Greek Bible the term becomes *ketos megalos,* which is the term also used in 3 Maccabees 6:8; Josephus, *Antiquities* 9.10.2; and Matthew 12: 40 for Jonah's fish. *Ketos* is a monster of undefined fish species, as is the Latin *piscis.* Nevertheless, a host of English versions of the New Testament follow the King James Version in rendering it "whale." The New English Bible, Phillips, American Revised Version margin and others have recognized that we need not identify the beast with a whale.

The continuous debate over whether there are fish in the Mediterranean that could swallow a man is actually beside the point since it is said that the Lord prepared the fish.

There are, of course, white sharks of adequate size to swallow a man while some species of the whale could not. More interesting is the question whether there are cases in which a man survived such an experience. *The Princeton Theological Review* XXV (Oct. 1927), page 636, cites the case of a certain James Bartley, which case has often been appealed to. The *Interpreter's Bible*, volume 6, page 874, denies that this is an authentic case and insists that there is no known case of a man swallowed by a fish and later being cast forth alive. The issue of the book of Jonah is not to be decided on whether Bartley was or was not swallowed.

The Converted Prophet

Jonah's experience with the storm and the fish converted him. The second command to preach against Ninevah was obeyed. Jonah arose, went to the city, entered in, and raised his cry which is eight words in Hebrew: "Yet forty days and Nineveh will be overthrown." A converted prophet made a powerful preacher. The effect upon the superstitious population was phenomenal. From the king on down the people repented, fasted, and sat in sackcloth and ashes. The psychology of fasting is to say to the Lord: "I am already humble. You need not afflict me further." Even the beasts were brought into the acts of penance (cf. Judith 4:10).

The Lord relented and did not the evil which he had threatened.

A City of Three Days' Journey

Nineveh, though an exceedingly old city, came to its heyday later than the time of Jonah and reached its peak under Sennacherib.

Nineveh is today represented by two mounds which are in Iraq across the Tigris River from the modern city of Mosul: Quyundijiq, a mound about one mile in length and 650 yards wide and 90 feet high, and Nebi Yunus, a smaller mound. Quyundijiq has been intermittently excavated since the time of Layard, now more than one hundred years ago, and the secrets of its palaces revealed. (See A. Parrot, *Nineveh and the Old Testament.*) Nebi Yunus has a Muslim cemetery and a modern village on it so that it cannot be extensively excavated. It is easy to trace out the defensive wall of the ancient city. The wall in appearance somewhat resembles a river levee of earth with breaks in it where gates were. The circumference of this wall is 7½ miles and a journey of 1½ miles would take one to the center of the enclosed area. One is left wondering what "a city of three days' journey in breadth" meant. Several efforts have been made to explain the phrase. One suggests that it means it would take three days to see the principal sights of the city, but the fact that Jonah went one day's journey into the city (Jonah 3:4) is not really favorable to this view. A second view attempts to bring the entire Assyrian triangle into the picture with Nineveh, Rehoboth-Ir, Calah, and Resen (Gen. 10:11 f.), which would, of course, give a very large area. We must admit that the phrase still puzzles us.

The Lesson of the Gourd Vine

Jonah's bitterness at the outcome of the affair was such that he would have been happier dead. He makes it quite plain that it was not preaching to Nineveh that he minded, nor the dangers and hardships of the journey, but it was the possibility that the people might repent and be spared that he resented. He was afraid of God's mercy, and that fear drove him to Tarshish. If he did not preach to Nineveh, then the people would not repent, and God would have no alternative but to destroy Nineveh.

Jonah, despite his wrath at the Lord's sparing Nineveh, built himself a booth on the east of the city to wait for the outcome. He is in the peculiar position of being a preacher who hoped that he would not succeed. The plant that the Lord caused to grow up pleased him no end, but made his anger all the more bitter when it was cut off by the worm. Ibn Ezra made quite plain that one does not have to know the species of the plant that shaded Jonah to understand its lesson.

It was at this point that the Lord called Jonah's attention to his concern for a comparatively worthless plant for which he had not labored. Could he not then understand God's concern for the 120,000 innocent people of Nineveh who knew neither right or wrong—doubtless infants—as well as the much cattle that God had created which, of course, were not capable of sin? The contrast of the whole is between Jonah's attitude to Nineveh and the Lord's attitude. Here in the plainest way is taught "God so loved the world." Traits of God comparable to those of Exodus 34:6 are emphasized.

Interpretation

A question in the interpretation of Jonah, second only to the "fish question," is that of the nature of the book. Is the book fiction, allegory, or history? As early as the eighteenth century it was proposed that Jonah (whose name means "dove" while Israel is compared to a dove, cf. Hos. 7:11; 11:11) represents the disobedient people of Israel who failed to carry God's message to the nations of the world. The sea represents the tossing heathen ready to engulf Israel. Israel is swallowed up by Babylon (cf. Jer. 51:34) and then spit out in the return from captivity (cf. Jer. 51:44). Obvious difficulties in this sort of interpretation are that it deals with only the first half of the book and neglects Jonah's journey to Nineveh and Nineveh's repentance. In addition no other Old Testament allegory is spun about a historical figure. It really has only the imagination to commend it.

More relevant is the question of history or fiction. Until fairly recent both Jew and Christian thought of the book as history. The need for a historical story seems bound up in the New Testament use of the book. The Bible believer has always felt that the comparison Jesus made between himself and Jonah demanded that Jonah be historical. The effort to say that Jesus was only a man of his day and accepted certain views prevalent among those about him carries implications that we are not ready to accept. This question is heatedly discussed by J. W. McGarvey in his book *Jesus and Jonah.*

The History of the Book

Jonah had already been accepted into the book of the twelve by the time of Sirach (Sir. 49:10). Small scraps of the book have been found in Cave 2 of Qumran, which would be the oldest text of the book in existence. It is also represented in the leather Greek text that has been found near the Dead Sea.

The story of Jonah is appealed to in Tobit 14:4 where Jonah's threat of the destruction of Nineveh is considered to be an unfulfilled prophecy that must be fulfilled. (This passage has a textual problem. Codex Sinaiticus reads "Nahum" rather than "Jonah.") In 3 Macc. 6:8, Jonah's deliverance is one in a series of God's great acts of mercy of the past that forms a part of the prayer of Eleazar. In his *Antiquities* 9.10.2, Josephus identifies the minor prophet with the prophet of 2 Kings 14:25 and summarizes the book, but neglects to mention its main theme of repentance.

Great Lessons from Jonah

1. The universality of God's presence. Compare Psalm 139:7-12; Amos 9:2-4; and the ideas of the localized God (1 Sam. 26:19 f.; 1 Kings 20:23, 28; 2 Kings 5:17 f.).

2. The universal concern of God for man. Compare Acts 10:34, 35; John 3:16.

3. The conditional nature of prophecy. Compare Jeremiah 18:7 f.

Jonah and the New Testament

The book of Jonah contains no Messianic predictions. At the same time Jesus directly compares his approaching experiences in the grave to those of Jonah in the fish (Matt. 12:

39 f.). That the resurrection on the third day is "according to scripture" (1 Cor. 15:4), may allude to Jonah's experience. The idea that Jesus was crucified on Friday requires that one interpret "three days and three nights" as portions of three units of time rather than as three periods of 24 hours each.

A second point is made in the New Testament in calling attention to the repentance of Nineveh at the preaching of Jonah; therefore Nineveh will condemn the Lord's generation in judgment: "A greater than Jonah is here" (Matt. 12:41).

DISCUSSION

1. Where is Tarshish?
2. Have we escaped from the idea of the localized God?
3. How is Jonah different from the other minor prophets?
4. What basis was there for Jonah's feeling toward Nineveh?
5. Can you find contrasts between the attitude of Jonah and that of other biblical figures?
6. How do you harmonize the theme of Jonah with the idea of God's having a chosen people?
7. What facts about the nature of prophecy are most clearly illustrated by Jonah?
8. How old is the book of Jonah?
9. Is one miracle more significant than another?
10. Does the fact that Jesus referred to Jonah prove conclusively that the book cannot be allegorical, parabolic, or fictional?

READINGS ON JONAH

McGarvey, J. W., *Jesus and Jonah* (reprint, Murfreesboro, Tennessee: Dehoff, 1952).

Aalders, G. Ch., *The Problem of the Book of Jonah* (London: Tyndale Press, 1948).

Chapter VI

THE PROPHET ZEPHANIAH

The Prophet

The name "Zephaniah" means "He whom Jehovah has hidden." The Greek and Latin Bibles call this prophet Sophonias. His book is ninth in the sequence of the minor prophets. While there are three men in the Old Testament with this name (1 Chron. 6:36; Jer. 21:1; Zeph. 1:1), there is no reason to connect the other two with the prophet.

Zephaniah traces his ancestry back four generations (Zeph. 1:1) and is the only prophet to do so. The reason is uncertain, but it has been conjectured that it is because his ancestor Hizkiah is to be identified with King Hezekiah. If so, it should be remembered that Zephaniah and Hezekiah are separated by about one hundred years.

It is often thought that the prophet lived in Jerusalem because of his detailed knowledge of conditions there, which knowledge is reflected in his book. Efforts to determine whether the prophet is old or young are entirely conjectural. Taking a hint from Zephaniah 1:12, artists of the Middle Ages regularly represented Zephaniah as the man with the lamp, searching Jerusalem for sinners to bring them to punishment. We have no further personal details about the prophet.

The Date

Zephaniah dates his oracles in the reign of Josiah (640-609 B.C.), thereby placing his activity in the late seventh century and making it possible that he was a contemporary of Jeremiah and of Huldah. He is perhaps slightly before the time of Nahum and Habakkuk, though one cannot be certain. The age of Josiah inherited a legacy of moral and religious degeneration from the days of Manasseh and Amon (2 Chron. 33:1-25; 2 Kings 21:1-26). Josiah came to the throne at the age of eight and in his 18th year, with the discovery of a copy of the law, carried out a sweeping reform. But the effort proved vain. The king lost his life in a futile attempt to prevent Pharaoh Necho from aiding Assyria in its dying struggles against rising Babylon. In a brief 34 years after the most thoroughgoing reform that Judah saw, Nebuchadnezzar had swept over Judah, exiled her people, imprisoned and blinded her king, destroyed her temple, and left Jerusalem a mere memory in the hearts of the survivors.

We are immediately confronted with the question of whether the book of Zephaniah was before or after the reform of Josiah in 621 B.C. (2 Kings 22-23; 2 Chron. 34:3 ff.). The reform of Josiah involved the suppression of idolatrous worship, some of which no doubt came about through Manasseh's servitude to Assyria (2 Kings 21:3-7). A careful study of the reform of Josiah and its significance should be undertaken as a preparation for the study of Zephaniah.

The fact that Zephaniah denounces foreign customs, worship of the heavenly bodies, religious syncretism, and practical skepticism makes some basis for the claim that the prophet precedes Josiah's reform. There is, however, no sound basis for assuming that his oracles played a part in that reform.

The Enemy

Prophetic activity was at times touched off by external circumstances. Joel and Amos saw plagues of locusts and from them prophesied. The most crucial question in the study of Zephaniah is that of the identity of the unnamed threatening power that is on the horizon. The prophet is quite emphatic that a nation threatens Judah, which threat he connects with the Day of the Lord.

It has been most popular to identify this nation with the

Scythians who broke out from near the Caucasus about 630 B.C. Herodotus (*The Histories* I.103-106) tells us of the Scythian invasion of the fertile crescent and of their pressing on down to the border of Egypt where they were bought off by Psammetichus I, king of Egypt. On their return they plundered the temple of Celestial Venus in Askelon. Herodotus tells us that their domination over Asia lasted 28 years. It is known that they joined the Medes and Babylonians in the destruction of Nineveh.

The Scythian hypothesis has played a very major role in the interpretation of both Jeremiah and Zephaniah. Its shortcoming is that as far as Judah is concerned, the Scythian menace never really materialized. Herodotus does not speak of an invasion of Judah. While Bethshean is called Scythopolis in an inscription of 218 B.C., there is no evidence that the name actually goes back to a Scythian invasion. With the publication of the records of the Neo-Babylonian empire, it is widely recognized that the time has come to abandon the Scythian hypothesis in the interpretation of Jeremiah. Perhaps the same is also true of Zephaniah. There is no valid reason to make a prophet predict an invasion that never materialized unless the evidence is conclusive that he did so.

Outline of the Book

The book of Zephaniah is arranged in a manner comparable to that of Isaiah, Jeremiah, and Ezekiel. There are three elements: (1) The prophet's own people are indicted. (2) There is a denunciation of foreign nations. (3) There is a vision of future glory for Israel.

A. 1:1-13. The Lord threatens to sweep the earth clean.

B. 1:14-18. The Day of the Lord.

C. 2:1-3. The Lord's mercy should lead to repentance.

D. 2:4-15. Prophecies against heathen nations: Gaza and the Philistine plain, Moab, Ammon, Ethiopia, and Assyria.

E. 3:1-20. The sin of Jerusalem and future salvation.

The Sins of Judah

1. Religious syncretism. Zephaniah attacks the nation for worshiping Baal (1:4), and Milcam (1:5) and the host of heaven (1:5), while at the same time bowing down and swearing by the Lord. These practices had been introduced and fostered by Ahaz and Manasseh (2 Kings 21:3, 5; 23:11 f.; cf. Jer. 7:17 f.).

2. Wearing of foreign apparel (1:8); leaping over the threshold (1:9; cf. 1 Sam. 5:5).

3. Fraud and violence (1:9).

4. Prophet, priest, and judge are condemned as violent, wanton men (3:3, 4).

5. A practical skepticism of indifference prevailed which insisted that the Lord was not concerned with human behaviour, either to reward or to punish (1:12). In contrast, the prophet insists that the Lord will do justly (3:5).

6. Jerusalem refuses to receive correction (3:2, 7). She has refused the lessons of history; she listens to no voice (3:2). The concept of correction (*musar*) also plays a vital role in the book of Jeremiah (5:3; 7:28; 32:33).

The Day of the Lord

The major theme of Zephaniah is the approaching Day of the Lord. Amos (5:18) is the first writing prophet specifically to use this phrase which must be older than Amos, and which seems to have been in popular expectation a day when all enemies would be put down and Israel and her God would be exalted. The prophets reinterpreted the phrase to be a day within history (as contrasted to a day at the end of history in which a nation would receive its doom; cf. Joel 1:15; 2:1; (Obad. 15).

Zephaniah plays no small role in the developing picture. There is first the sacrificial feast imagery in which the invited guests are the nations—the Lord's agents in the calamity. The victims are the members of the royal house who are guilty of violence (Zeph. 1:7, 8), but all who are guilty of

syncretism and of indifference will also suffer (1:8-12). These
are to be searched out for punishment as one searches with a
lamp (1:12). Near this time Jeremiah was searching Jerusalem
for a righteous man that the city might be spared (Jer. 5:1).
A cry goes up from the various quarters of the city where
commercial activities have been carried on (Zeph. 1:10, 11).

The day is near at hand. In gripping poetry in which one
can feel the very foundations of earth quaking, Zephaniah
describes the terrors of the day affecting man, beast, bird,
and fish (1:2, 3). "A day of wrath is that day, a day of dis-
tress and anguish, a day of ruin and devastation, a day of
darkness and gloom, a day of clouds and thick darkness, a
day of trumpet blast and battle cry against the fortified cities
and the lofty battlements" (1:15, 16). It is a day of wrath of
the Lord from which neither silver nor gold can deliver (1:
18), and life is counted as worthless as dung (1:17).

Zephaniah's Day of the Lord played an important role in
the forming of the concept of the final judgment day. At
times it is difficult to avoid feeling that he is speaking of the
final day (e.g., 1:2, 3; 3:8). In particular the Vulgate version
is the inspiration of the medieval hymn by Thomas of Celano
(A.D. 1250), *Dies irae, dies illa,* which has been translated
into numerous languages, the opening lines of which are:

> O day of wrath, O day of mourning.
> See fulfilled the prophet's warning.
> Heaven and earth in ashes burning.

The Nations

The judgment that Zephaniah sees upon Judah enlarges
itself to include the nations. It is distinctive that Zephaniah
has not one word of denunciation of sin or crime on the part
of the nations except for Moab and for Nineveh whose sin
seems to be that of taunts (2:8, 10) and of pride (2:15).
While the Philistines and Nineveh felt the blow of the Scythians, the presence of the other nations in the denunciation

makes clear that the passage is not limited to the Scythian threat.

The prophet threatens the Philistine plain, beginning with a pun on Gaza—Gaza shall be forsaken (*Azzah—azubah*)— and upon Ekron—Ekron shall be rooted up (*'eqron-te'aqer*)— but Ashdod and Askelon are also mentioned as are the Cherethites who are one clan of the Philistines (cf. Ezek. 25:16; 2 Sam. 8:18).

Zephaniah next turns attention to Ammon and Moab, threatening that they will become like Sodom and Gomorrah, to be plundered by the "remnant of my people" (2:8, 9). Next are the Ethiopians (2:12), which threat probably finds fulfillment when Nebuchadnezzar conquered Egypt in the 38th year of his reign (568 B.C.).

Particularly severe are the denunciations against Nineveh, which is to become a desolation and the object of a hiss of scorn to all who pass by (2:13-15). The fall of Nineveh came in 612 B.C. The student should also read Nahum and the material on Nineveh suggested in that lesson of this series.

The Alternative to Destruction

Like most of the prophets, Zephaniah has an alternative to offer to the destruction he threatens. The meek of the earth who seek the Lord in humility and righteousness may be hidden on the day of the wrath of the Lord (2:3). Further stress on humility is to be seen in Chapter 3:11, 12.

It is to be noticed that his is not a general call to repentance that can turn aside the calamity. It would seem that the day of grace is already passed. Doom awaits. There is no hope of recovery, but only that some may escape.

After the Calamity

Nevertheless, as has been implied, Zephaniah's day is within the framework of history. He promises a restoration of the fortunes of Judah, which remnant will possess the land of the Philistines (2:7) as well as the land of Ammon and Moab

(2:9). It should be noticed that this better age is not the result of social reform, but of God's action in judgment. The doctrine of the remnant is also to be found in Amos, Hosea, Isaiah, and Jeremiah. Zephaniah envisions a people of pure speech who will call on the name of the Lord and serve him with one accord (3:9). None will make them afraid (3:13). Israel will no longer be haughty on the Lord's holy mountain (3:11). Jehovah is king in her midst. The prophet envisions no specific Messianic king (3:14-17), but all nations will worship God (3:9, 10).

DISCUSSION

1. Can it be legitimately contended that the expectation of Zephaniah was fulfilled in the return from captivity, or is this an unfulfilled prophecy?
2. What have the times of Zephaniah in common with our own times?
3. What spiritual condition contains the greatest threat to the Lord's cause?
4. Has the Day of the Lord of Zephaniah been correctly interpreted in the lesson material when it is thought of as a day within history?
5. Did Zephaniah envision the Scythians as the instruments of God's wrath?
6. What well-known figure of the times of the end makes its appearance in Zephaniah? Where else in Scripture is it to be found?
7. What is it to be "settled on their lees"?
8. What emphasis upon the mercy of God is there in Zephaniah?
9. What traits of God are stressed? What is your specific evidence?
10. What is the lesson of calamities of the past as presented by Zephaniah?

Chapter VII

THE PROPHET NAHUM

The Prophet

About the prophet Nahum, the seventh in order of the twelve prophets, we know only his name and the name of his town, Elkosh. The location of Elkosh is another matter. Jerome (*Prol. in Nahum*) placed it in Galilee at Elkese; Capernaum means "village of Nahum"; while Ps.-Epiphanius (*De vitis prophetarum* 17) located it in Judah near Eleutheropolis, 20 miles S.W. of Jerusalem. Benjamin of Tudela in the twelfth century claimed to have seen his tomb south of Babylon. Since the sixteenth century a place 24 miles north of Mosul, Iraq, called Al-Kush has been pointed out, and the tomb of the prophet revered. This latter tradition would make Nahum a descendant of the Northern tribes (2 Kings 17:6); however, Al-Kush is not an ancient site. There is really slight evidence for any of the identifications. The name Nahum means "comfort" or "compassion."

Calls, visions, and experiences of the prophet play no part in this book. Even his date has been greatly disputed with guesses running all the way from 650 B.C. to after 612 B.C. The allusion to the capture of Thebes (Nah. 3:8) would prevent the book from being earlier, for Egypt was entered by Esarhaddon about 670 B.C. and Thebes was perhaps taken by Ashurbanipal about 667 B.C. and finally destroyed by the latter about 661 B.C.

Though some have argued that Nahum was written after the fall of Nineveh, it would seem more likely that the book is just before the fall, or about 612 B.C. The events are fresh and hot. Nahum is then to be thought of as a prophet of the seventh century B.C. and a contemporary of the early career

of Jeremiah, as well as not greatly removed in time from
Zephaniah and Habakkuk.

The Theme

The theme of Nahum is the overthrow of Nineveh. Its
spirit of revenge and rejoicing is in marked contrast to the
theme of the book of Jonah, which also deals with Nineveh.
In the book of Jonah, God forgave Nineveh; in Nahum he
announces and executes its doom. Nahum rejoices over its
downfall as Jonah would have done had his threats been
carried out; however, it is the recognition of the just judgment
of God rather than sheer vengefulness. "At last," the prophet
shouts, for the fall of Nineveh brings relief for Judah (Nah.
1:12, 13, 15; 2:2). It is a cry of outraged humanity as there
are other cries against Assyria in Isaiah 30:30, 31; and Zephaniah 2:13-15. Nahum, in its general theme of victory over
an enemy, might be compared to the song of Deborah (Judg.
5). To understand this attitude, it is necessary to study the
history of Nineveh and to consider what the Assyrian conquest meant.

Nineveh

Asshur, 50 miles south of Nineveh, was the original capital of Assyria. How long Nineveh served is unknown, but
perhaps from the beginning of Sennacherib's supremacy to
the fall of the state, or about 98 years. However, the town is
much older. Its foundation is traced back to Asshur (KJV:
Gen. 10:11; modern commentators take the subject of the
verb to be Nimrod), but Sennacherib planned its fortifica-
tions, restored its temples, and gave it a system of water-
works. He built a large platform for his palace. Perhaps as
many as 10,000 men worked for twelve years to deposit the
15,000,000 tons of earth and brick required. In Assyrian art
the slaves are clothed in short tunics. It is not impossible that
Israelite deportees (2 Kings 18:13-16) may have furnished a
part of the force.

Today the remains of Nineveh lie across the Tigris River
from Mosul and are about 1500 yards from the river, though
in ancient times the river may have been nearer. Despite the
fact that Diodorus Siculus describes a wall of a circuit of
60 miles, an area of about 7½ miles' circuit is enclosed in the
existing earthen defensive walls. The wall is interrupted here
and there by breaks that represent the fifteen gates. Only one
gate, the northern one, has been restored in its former location with its protective winged bull.

Two mounds remain. Quyundjiq has been subjected to repeated excavation by Layard, Rassam, Place, and a host of
others over the past 100 years, revealing the treasures of the
Assyrian kings, which have since been carted off to the various
museums of the world. Today there is only waste on this
impressive mound that is about one mile long and 650 yards
wide and 90 feet high. Upon it has been built a water tank to
give pressure to the water supply in the nearby village. Nebi
Yunus, the other mound of Nineveh, is separated from Quyundjiq by a small river, the Khoser. On it there is a cemetery
and a village so that excavation is impossible. The growing
village slowly encroaches on the area once enclosed by
Nineveh while fields and the tin cans of the city dump cover
other sections.

Assyria, of which Nineveh was the capital, was a nation
largely geared for aggressive war. Its atrocities were proverbial as the records and the art left by its kings make quite
clear. Though it could conquer the world, it proved unable
to rule it. Its victims lay prone under tyranny, but no national spirit breathed in the corpus. No peace organization
of any proper kind existed to keep the whole together.
Nineveh saw men and nations as tools to be exploited to
gratify the lust of conquest and commercialism. Assyria existed to render no service to mankind.

The relations of Israel and Judah to Assyria may be
described as "From Qarqar to Carchemish." At Qarqar Ahab
and his allies first fought Shalmaneser III in 853 B.C. and
Israel shortly thereafter became tributary and was finally
destroyed in 722 B.C. Judah became tributary under Ahab in

735 B.C.; was threatened by Sargon in 711 B.C. (cf. Isa. 20);
and was pulverized by Sennacherib in 701 B.C., though she
barely escaped through the destruction of Sennacherib's army
(2 Kings 18:13–19:36). Nineveh fell in 612 B.C. but a rump
state at Haran continued until defeated by Nebuchadnezzar
at Carchemish in 606 B.C.

Assyria reached its peak under Ashurbanipal who, though
most widely known for his library, was also its last great
ruler. Following his death in 626 B.C. the downfall came
swiftly. Assyrian records are lacking for the last 25 years of
Nineveh's existence, but from classical sources and the Babylonian Chronicle the details can be filled in. As early as 625
B.C., Cyaxares may have been attacking Nineveh. But Nineveh fell before the onslaught of a combined thrust by
Babylonians under Nabopolassar, by the Medes led by Cyaxares, and by the Scythians. The destruction was so complete
that when Xenophon and his 10,000 Greeks passed by the site
some 200 years later they gave no indication of knowing that
the capital had existed.

The Structure of the Book

Nahum's book is comprised of three chapters. After the
introductory verse (1:1) the book falls into two sections, the
first of which (Chap. 1) deals with a theophany—the coming
of the Lord in judgment—before whose wrath the physical
world trembles, while the second (Chaps. 2 and 3) describes
in vivid details the downfall of Nineveh despite its frenzied
defense. The book ends with an epitaph to Nineveh (3:18 f.).

The book announces that it is a "burden against Nineveh."
"Burden" is a technical word meaning "oracle against." The
double heading (1:1) as well as the occurrence of "book" in
a heading is unique to this prophet. It has been thought that
Chapter 1 is in part an acrostic poem; however, the entire
alphabet cannot be traced out and some of the letters are not
in proper order. Other examples of acrostics are to be found
in Psalms 25, 34, 111, 112, 119, and 145.

In Chapters 2 and 3 naked ideas are presented with all possible force: "Defenses manned!" "Road watched!" "Loins girded!" In excellent poetry the calamity is presented. The elegiac meter with a rhythm of three stresses in the first half of the line and two in the second (there are exceptions) is used. The book should be read carefully to observe its force of expression. Two sections begin with "I am against thee" (2:13; 3:5).

Sins

Nahum has nothing to say concerning sins of Judah. He has no threats of punishment for her nor any promise of a golden age of peace and righteousness. Even his thoughts about Jehovah are not new. He is entirely taken up with the downfall of Nineveh and what it implies. Nineveh's fall, though carried out by her enemies, is really the judgment of God upon her sins. "I am against thee saith the Lord of Hosts," is twice repeated (2:13; 3:5). The sins of Nineveh that are specified are her atrocities, her idolatory, and her commercialism. This brutality is amply attested to in both literature and art (cf. Isa. 10:14).

The Vengeance of God

Nahum's major idea may really be put in the words "Vengeance is mine, I will repay, says the Lord." Nineveh has run roughshod over the nations, but "they who take the sword shall perish by the sword" (Matt. 26:52). Though none could withstand her, God, who rules in the kingdoms of men, can and will bring her down.

Though God is slow to anger and abundant in loving-kindness (as his action toward Nineveh in the book of Jonah shows), his long-suffering is not to be interpreted as indifference or as lack of power (Nah. 1:1-6). He is also full of wrath and indignation. When he goes into action, none can resist him and he has decreed the end of Nineveh (1:6, 8-14).

"The face of the Lord is against them that do evil to cut off the remembrance of them from the earth" (Ps. 34:16).

God is also a stronghold in time of trouble to those who trust in him (Nah. 1:7). His decree of the end of Ninevah is good news to Judah (1:15). Though the New Testament speaks of the beauty of the feet of those who bring good news (Acts 10:36; Rom. 10:15), it is more likely an echo of Isaiah 40:9; 52:7 than of Nahum 1:15.

The End of Nineveh

The enemy is unnamed, but the attack and frenzied defense of Nineveh are described. Chariots dash in the streets (2:4). The call to stand finds no response (2:8). Spoil is abundant (2:9). In irony it is asked, Where is the dwelling of the lions (the national symbol of Assyria) where the lion and the whelps devoured the prey and none made them afraid (2:11)? The lion filled his den with prey, but now the processes are reversed. Though the enemy executes the deed, it is really the Lord who is her attacker (2:13).

The poet returns in Chapter 3 to his description. The rattling chariots, jumping horses, and multitude of slain come into view (3:1-3). The harlot (Nineveh) will be stripped and filth thrown at her (3:4-6). Nineveh is no more exempt from danger than was Thebes, which Ashurbanipal had overthrown. Thebes is 400 miles south of Cairo, and though populous and protected by seas and faithful allies, she went into captivity. Nineveh will be no more secure than ripe figs when shaken from a tree. Her people are no more forceful than women (3:8-13). In irony the prophet calls for defense activity: drawing water and making brick (3:14).

In a final taunt the prophet compares the stability of Nineveh's leaders to locusts that settle on a hedge on a cold day, but which depart in every direction when the sun comes out. Assyria's shepherds slumber, her people are scattered with none to gather them (3:18).

The wound is beyond healing. This is the end for Nineveh. All that hear of her fate will clap their hands (3:19).

Text

Fragments of a commentary on Nahum 2:11-13 were found in Cave 1 at Qumran near the Dead Sea and would be the earliest witnesses to the text of the book. The community applied the phrases of Nahum to problems arising following the Greek period and to evils in Jerusalem. This prophet is not cited or echoed in the New Testament.

Great Ideas of Nahum

1. God rules in the kingdoms of men.
2. God is a stronghold in the time of trouble (Nah. 1:7).
3. There are no strongholds secure from the vengeance of God.
4. "The history of the world is the judgment of the world," said Schiller. Nations mete out judgment to nations. Nations reap what they sow and the wages of sin is death. Nahum is a book of relevance in a world of dictators.
5. The end of God's patience.

DISCUSSION

1. Is Nahum's doctrine of God's providence in history relevant to present day international problems?
2. Is the joy Nahum shows over the fall of Nineveh lacking in Christian spirit?
3. What traits of God are called to our attention by Nahum?
4. What is the difference between the role of Assyria as seen by Isaiah (ch. 10) and that presented by Nahum?
5. Can a man love good if he does not hate injustice and evil?
6. Describe the contribution of Nineveh to biblical history.
7. Should Nahum be in any sense considered an unfulfilled prophecy?
8. What can be known of Nahum as a person?
9. What features unique to this prophet does the book of Nahum present?
10. What figures of speech are used in the book to describe Nineveh?

Chapter VIII

THE PROPHET HABAKKUK

The Prophet

The third of the seventh century B.C. prophets and the eighth in sequence in the total collection of minor prophets is Habakkuk. Though we are not absolutely certain of the date of his activity, the prophet seems to have prophesied shortly before the rise of the Babylonians to power. The wrongs suffered under Jehoiachim (608-597 B.C.) have been thought by some to be those of which the prophet complains (cf. Jer. 22:13-19). The prophet is perhaps a contemporary of Jeremiah and Zephaniah and only slightly later than Nahum.

The prophet's name is not of Hebrew origin, but may be traced to a root meaning "to embrace" as Jerome and Luther thought, or it may go back to the name of an Assyrian flower. The name does not occur outside of the book.

Nothing certain can be known about the prophet as a person. He describes himself as "the prophet" (*ha-nabi*; Hab. 1:1), which though unusual is also used in their books for Haggai and Zechariah. In rabbinic tradition he is made to be the son of the Shunamite woman (2 Kings 4:16 f.) and he is said to have fled to Egypt after Nebuchadnezzar captured Jerusalem in 586 B.C. Further legendary material may also be gleaned in the Apocrypha from *Bel and the Dragon* 33-39 where he is connected with the tribe of Levi and is carried by the hair of his head by the angel of the Lord to Babylon to supply Daniel with pottage when the latter is in the lion's den.

Literary Form

The book of Habakkuk, a book of excellent poetic form, is written in the style of a complaint and an answer. In contrast to the other prophets who addressed themselves to Israel in order to declare the will of God, this prophet addresses himself to God on behalf of Israel. He does not exercise himself concerning the sins of his people. His is an effort to justify the ways of God to man. It is a book of consolation to a people upon whom the threatening shadow of long exile was rapidly sinking.

Following the title in Habakkuk 1:1, the book has three major divisions:

1. Habakkuk 1:2-11. Habakkuk presents his problem: How can God allow lawlessness to go unchecked? How long will it go on? The answer given is that God is raising up the Chaldeans to take care of the evil doers.

2. Habakkuk 1:12—2:20. Habakkuk is now confronted with a new problem. How can God use such cruel power to punish a people less wicked than are the Chaldeans? The answer comes in Chapter 2:1-4. The wicked man will not last. Evil is self-destructive but the righteous man will live by faithfulness. There follows a series of woes upon the aggressor.

3. Chapter 3 is a poem with musical notations in which there are two divisions: verses 1-16 describe a vision of God's appearance for judgment; verses 17-19 are a hymn of faith.

The Ways of God

Every man raises questions of the justice of God (or of life itself, which is the same question) when he falls into adversity: "Why did it happen to me?" Even when he admits he is evil, he asks, "Am I this evil? Do I deserve all this?" In a setting where one postulates the omnipotence, the monotheism, and the justice of God, the problem becomes all the more acute.

In Jewish literature the problem of theodicy (the justice of God) is frequently dealt with. The best known of these is the book of Job, which discusses the question of why does the individual righteous man suffer. But it is also the topic of Psalms 37, 49, 73, and Jeremiah 12:1.

There are at least two discussions of this problem—though they are upon the national rather than the individual level—in the noncanonical literature that are beneficial to study. These were probably written in the time of despair following A.D. 70. The book of 4 Ezra 3:29-36, while presenting the problem of the present under forms of the past, admits that Zion has sinned, but questions, Are the deeds of Babylon any better? The writer admits that individual righteous men may be found, but "nations thou shalt not find." The final answer of the book is that God's ways are inscrutable. Even more despair is to be seen in 2 Baruch 11:1-7 in which the writer declares that had Zion and Babylon prospered equally it would have been grievous, but now that Zion is desolate and Babylon prospers, grief is infinite. He wishes that the earth had ears to go proclaim to the dead "Blessed are ye more than we who live."

It is this same problem, of how one can justify the facts of life with the doctrine of an all-powerful but just God who is active in history, that Habakkuk discusses. Events do not seem to bear out the doctrine that sin brings retribution. God seems inactive.

The Chaldeans

Detailed information on the relationship between Judah and Babylon is to be found in A. Parrot, *Babylon and the Old Testament* (London: SCM Press, 1958). The Chaldeans are a tribe of Semites from Southern Babylonia who freed themselves from Assyrian overlordship in 625 B.C. and who under the leadership of Nabopolassar became rulers of the Neo-Babylonian empire. Joining with the Medes and Scythians, they destroyed Nineveh in 612 B.C. Josiah in 609 B.C. had lost his life at Megiddo vainly attempting to block Necho's advance to aid the dying Assyrian empire (2 Kings 23:29, 30). At Carchemish in 606 B.C. (cf. Jer. 46:2) the remnant of

Assyria and Pharaoh Necho were defeated by Nebuchadnezzar and Babylon's domination over Judah was assured. The new Babylonian Chronicle makes it likely that Nebuchadnezzar returned to Syria following his coronation and took tribute. These events furnish the background of Habakkuk's expectation from the Chaldeans.

The Neo-Babylonian empire with Nebuchadnezzar at its head dismembered Judah. In 597 B.C. Jehoiachin and a number of artisans were exiled. In 586 B.C. Jerusalem was destroyed. The time span of the empire is actually coextensive with the exile. By 539 B.C. Cyrus had conquered Babylon and the Persian period of biblical history sets in.

How Long?

Habakkuk asks, "How long?" rather than "Why?" How long will God allow violence and destruction to go unchecked (1:1-4)? Complaints to the Lord have gone unheeded. We are not informed whether it is of civil violence he complains or of oppression from a foreign oppressor.

The prophet is informed that God is not idle. He is doing a work that is beyond the scope of the prophet's mental horizon. God is raising up the Chaldeans to deal with the problem (cf. Isa. 10:5). In vivid details the violence of the Chaldeans is described (Hab. 1:6-11). Their horses are swifter than vultures; they gather captives like sand; their might is their god. They will take care of the violent against whom the prophet raises his complaint.

The prophet is only further perplexed. He admits that God has ordained the Chaldean for chastisement, but God is righteous and cannot look on wrong. How then can he stand by while a more righteous nation is swallowed by a less righteous one (1:12-17)? What has God to do with a nation that solely recognizes force?

The prophet takes his place on his watchtower to wait out the answer (2:1). The Lord orders him to write the answer plainly that it may be read at a hurried glance. The man whose soul is not upright within him shall fall. Wickedness will destroy itself. It will burst as a bubble; it will collapse as a wall; but the righteous man will live by his faithfulness. Running the universe is God's business. The righteous man has his daily tasks to fulfill, and by them he will live.

The prophet then issues a series of five woes against conquering nations (2:6 ff.): (1) Woe upon the plunderer, for he, himself, shall be plundered. (2) Woe upon him who thinks only of individual gain, for he forfeits his own soul. (3) Woe to him that oppresses others. Cities built by violence shall be destroyed. (4) Woe to him that reduces a people to helplessness. The violence will come home to him. (5) Woe to him who resorts to idolatry. The idol cannot save him, but the Lord is in his holy temple and all should keep silent before him.

The Psalm

Chapter 3 of Habakkuk is a psalm with musical notations, including three occurrences of the word *selah* such as are found in the book of Psalms. The chapter is used in the synagogue on Pentecost. The Lord is beseeched to go into action "in the midst of the years" (to contrast with the former times and the end times). In vivid poetic terms the coming of the Lord and its impact are described. The very thought of it causes the prophet to tremble in his boots.

The prophet closes his poems with one of the greatest declarations of faith to be found in biblical literature. Too many people's faith is "Lord, take care of me and I will take care of you." In contrast, the prophet who has raised such searching questions in the early part of the book declares that come the worst if it will, he will hold steadfastly to the Lord (cf. Job 13:15).

Qumran and Habakkuk

In 1947 in Cave 1 of Qumran near the Dead Sea, the Bedouin discovered a manuscript that is a commentary on Habakkuk. This manuscript dating from the first century

B.C. gives us our oldest copy of the book. Only the first two chapters are in the manuscript. There are only three lines of material in the last column of text and the remainder is blank, which would seem to imply that the omission is not accidental and that the community knew a shorter book than our book.

The commentary is of the type of exegesis that has come to be known as *midrash pesher,* meaning that it quotes the verse and then says: "The explanation of this is . . ." and proceeds to apply the description of Habakkuk to problems current to the community. It is in this material that we encounter the Teacher of Righteousness who is opposed by the Wicked Priest. A sizable library could be assembled out of the conjectural literature that has grown up over the question of the identity of these two figures. The opposing nation is called the "Kittim," and here again conjectures on the part of current interpreters are legion. Paper-bound English translations of the commentary by T. H. Gaster (*The Dead Sea Scriptures*) or by G. Vermes (*The Dead Sea Scrolls in English*) are available.

The New Testament and Habakkuk

Like many of the minor prophets, Habakkuk has no specific statements dealing with the person of the Messiah. The New Testament writers, however, sometimes found Old Testament phrases suitable to describe the situation that they confronted. Habakkuk 1:5 furnishes words to describe the perplexity caused by the opportunity afforded by the gospel (Acts 13:41).

A further item of influence from the prophet is Habakkuk 2:14 where he speaks of an earth full of knowledge of the Lord as waters cover the sea (cf. Isa. 11:9). Though not explicitly alluded to in the New Testament, this idea beautifully expresses the ideal of the gospel.

It is in his declaration that the just shall live by his faithfulness (*emunah*: Hab. 2:4)—that is, the Israelite who remains unswerving in his loyalty to moral principles, though he may suffer, will survive—that Habakkuk becomes most influential. Three times in the New Testament the passage is echoed: Romans 1:17; Galatians 3:11; Hebrews 10:37, 38. In the thought of Paul, justification by faith takes as its antithesis justification by the law.

Luther further developed the idea to make the key thought of the Reformation to be justification by faith only. This introduces a new idea that is neither in Habakkuk nor in Paul from whom Luther took his cue.

DISCUSSION

1. Have you ever asked Habakkuk's "Why?" Under what specific circumstances?
2. Are we to believe that God today punishes nations with other nations? Is it possible to predict God's alignment in present conflicts?
3. What significant song takes its inspiration from Habakkuk? What do the words mean in their setting?
4. What is the distinctive thing about the style of Habakkuk?
5. What is the proper attitude of the Christian in the face of ruthless power?
6. What common proverb describing a matter that is easy to understand do we owe to Habakkuk?
7. Can we really believe that evil has within it the germs of its own defeat?
8. What traits of God which we postulate and which are taught in Scripture make the "Why" more acute?
9. Is it sinful for a man to raise questions?
10. What are the minimum conditions under which you would be willing to serve the Lord?

Chapter IX

THE PROPHET HAGGAI

The Career of the Prophet

The first of the three post-exilic prophets known to us and the tenth in sequence of minor prophets, Haggai has a name that means "the joyous one" or "the festive one." It has been conjectured that the name implies that he was born on a festival. Though he is designated "the prophet" (Hag. 1:1; Ezra 5:1; 6:14), nothing certain is known of the prophet beyond that which can be deduced from his book and from the two references to him in Ezra 5:1 and 6:14 which make clear his role in completing the temple. Since the book of Ezra furnishes the background of Haggai, that book should be studied along with the book of Haggai.

In the LXX version (this Greek translation—the Septuagint—was made about 250 B.C. ff. in Alexandria) certain Psalms (Pss. 138 and 146-149) have the name of Haggai in their headings. In the Midrash and Talmud, legend makes Haggai, Zechariah, and Malachi to be the founders of the "Great Synagogue" (*Aboth R. Nathan* 1; *Baba Bathra* 15a), a body that is alleged to have played a great role in post-exilic times in preserving Scripture and handing on the traditional precepts and lore. It is further believed by the rabbis that after these three prophets died the Holy Spirit departed from Israel.

The work of Haggai, who is a contemporary of Zechariah, spread out over four months in the year 520 B.C. The exile had come to an end 16 years before. Haggai is in reality a man of one idea and that idea is: The temple must be completed! An age revolting against institutional worship and

67

drunk on the idea of "spiritual worship" should not attempt
to whittle Haggai down to its size. It must be admitted that
the temple played a most significant role in the history of
God's people. Haggai could see the duty next at hand and
enlisted men to accomplish it. After studying the earlier
prophets one must be impressed with the absence of denunciations of immorality, idolatry, and social injustice in the book
of Haggai. The moral conduct of man is not dealt with at
all.

The Persian Period

Cyrus II came to the throne of Anshan about 559 B.C. and,
after establishing his sovereignty over the Medes, finally peace-
ably took Babylon on October 13, 539 B.C. and "clasped the
hand [a phrase which means to become his worshiper] of
Marduck," god of Babylon. In this way the Neo-Bablyonian
Empire came to an end and the period of Persian domination
set in.

The *Nabonaid Chronicle* and the *Cyrus Cylinder* are our
most significant extra-biblical sources of information for the
events of this period. The *Nabonaid Chronicle* is a clay tab-
let now in the British Museum which relates the activities of
the last king of Babylon and the capture of Babylon by
Cyrus. The *Cyrus Cylinder* is a baked clay cylinder about
nine inches long found in Babylon by Rassam, also now to be
seen in the British Museum. It contains an account of Cyrus'
conquest of Babylon and of his policy of allowing captive
peoples to return to their native lands and rebuild their an-
cestral temples. The Persians were humane conquerors. Babylon was not destroyed. The policy of exiling peoples followed
by the Assyrians and Babylonians was reversed. Isaiah 45:1
points to Cyrus as the agent of the Lord to accomplish the
return from captivity. The statement of Josephus (*Ant.* 11.1,
2) that Cyrus had read Isaiah seems to be merely a conjecture on the part of Josephus. The records of Cyrus pre-
served outside the Bible do not specifically mention decrees
in favor of the Jews. Nevertheless, the *Cyrus Cylinder* makes

clear that it was a part of Cyrus' policy to allow subject
peoples to return home and to rebuild their temples. The per-
mission to the Jews alluded to in Ezra 1 would be in harmony
with this policy. Rather than being a believer in the Lord,
Cyrus, as the cylinder makes quite clear, like most ancient
people, was broad-minded on religious questions. He hoped
that prayer to all the gods would be offered for him. Under
these conditions the first return took place.

Cyrus was succeeded on the throne by his son Cambyses
(529-522 B.C.). Though Cambyses added Egypt to Persian
domains, he is not of major interest to the biblical student.
Darius I (521-486 B.C.), son of Hystaspes and next in the
sequence, represents a dynasty change. It was he who had
carved the well-known Behistun Rock to celebrate his victory
over rebels led by Gaumata during the early part of his reign.
It was this stone that gave the key to the cuneiform languages
to scholars. It was during the second year of Darius that
Haggai was active. The effect of his prophecy is seen in the
fact that the temple was completed and dedicated in 516
B.C. (the sixth year of Darius) (Ezra 6:15).

These early Persian rulers were followed by Xerxes (perhaps Ahasuerus) and Artaxerxes I before the Old Testament
story comes to an end.

The Returns from Captivity

Just as the departure into captivity took place in stages, so
also the return took place in at least three stages: (1) In 536
B.C. Sheshbazzar led back a group of about 50,000 persons to
Jerusalem (Ezra 2). Some Jews remained in Babylon (Josephus, *Ant.* 11.1.3) but made contributions to the under-
taking. During the period of exile they had built houses and
married (Jer. 29:5, 6). They had gone into business. On the
other hand conditions in Judah were unsatisfactory and the
trip was dangerous (Josephus, *Ant.* 11.1, 3 f.). Other passages
would inform us that Zerubbabel played an important role in
this return. Jewish tradition would identify Sheshbazzar and
Zerubbabel. Many today would make them successive to each

other. We are not certain of their relationship. Joshua, the priest, served as the religious leader of the returned group. (2) In 457 B.C. when 79 years had gone by, Ezra led back a second group composed of about 2,058 persons (Ezra 8:1-34) and accomplished reforms, particularly in regard to inter-marriage. (3) In 445 B.C., 13 years after Ezra's return, Nehemiah returned with a third group (Neh. 2). Nehemiah made at least two trips to Jerusalem and served as its governor.

The Persian period continued until the conquests of Alexander the Great. Persia fell to Alexander at the battle of Gaugamela in 331 B.C. This event takes us beyond the time of the minor prophets and into the period of intertestamental history.

The Temple

The people of the first return found the temple in ruins to which state it had been reduced by the Babylonians in 586 B. C. (2 Kings 25:9). Promptly the altar was set up in its place and sacrifice was resumed. Amid shouts and tears of joy the foundations of a new temple were laid (Ezra 3:12; 5:16). The offer of help from the people in Palestine who had not been in exile was bluntly refused (Ezra 4:3) and these in turn frustrated the work by complaining to Persian officials that the Jews were rebellious people (Ezra 4:4, 5). The work ground to a halt and so remained for 16 years while a spirit of indifference and defeatism predominated. It is to this problem that Haggai speaks.

The Book

Haggai's brief book of two chapters totaling 38 verses consists of four oracles all delivered in the second year of Darius Hystaspes, which is 520 B.C. These oracles obviously have as their purpose to stir the people from their lethargy and indifference and to urge them to rebuild the temple.

Oracle one, dating about August 29, 520 B.C., urges that the time for rebuilding the temple is long overdue (Hag. 1:2-11). The reasons for the delay may be read between the lines. Perhaps some said that the 70 years of the captivity were not yet complete (Jer. 25:11). Others may have pointed to the opposition of the people of the land or appealed to the poverty of the community, but more prominent is the fact that an indifference had arisen which made the people content to build their own houses while the Lord's house was neglected (Hag. 1:4). Warnings from God in the form of drought and want had gone unheeded (1:6, 11). The people were accustoming themselves to live without a temple. The prophet urges them to put the temple first in their plans. "Consider your ways" (1:7). The problem is not in times and conditions but in your own hearts, the prophet implies (cf. Matt. 6:33).

The result of the prophet's warnings is that 24 days later the people, led by Zerubbabel and Joshua, set to work on the temple (Hag. 1:12, 14), while the prophet assures them that the Lord is with them (1:13).

The second oracle (2:1-9) uttered at the feast of Tabernacles, October, 520 B.C. (21st day of the seventh month), dates two months later than the first (2:1 ff.). The oracle has as its major purpose the encouragement of those who tended to compare the second temple with the first. Sixty-six years have lapsed since the destruction of the first temple, yet some survived that had seen it. The second, although the dimensions are comparable (60 cubits wide and 60 cubits high; Ezra 6:3), did not compare favorably. After all, the returned community was not as rich as Solomon (cf. 1 Kings 10:27).

The Lord promises the wealth of the nations to glorify the temple. Two interesting items are here found: (1) "The desire of the nations" (Hag. 2:7) was taken by the rabbis to be the Messiah. This interpretation was borrowed from them by such scholars as Jerome. Some have seen it predicting Christ's visits to the temple. However, the verb in Hebrew is plural. Neither does the LXX version justify the use of a singular verb here. It is likely, despite the long-standing interpretation, that this is not a Messianic passage, but should be understood as "choice treasures of the Gentiles" (cf. 1 Sam. 9:20; Isa. 60:5). Gifts were received from Darius (Ezra 6:9-13), Artaxerxes (Ezra 7:12-26), as well as other Gentiles (2 Macc. 3:3). (2) The latter glory is to exceed the former (Hag. 2:9). If the comparison is between Solomon's temple and Zerubbabel's temple, it really cannot be. Homiletically the rabbis made the first temple exceed the second in five items (T. B. *Yoma* 21b): The second had no ark of the covenant, breastplate of gems, cloud of glory, fire from heaven, and spirit of prophecy. What the Hebrew text really says is that the latter glory of the house shall be greater than the former (that is, than it is now at its beginning). The rendering of the King James Version introduces a false comparison. The prophet also promises peace (Hag. 2:9).

Oracle three (2:10-19) was uttered on the 24th of the ninth month (December 520 B.C.), two months after the second, and is perhaps a reply to those who felt that God's blessings were slow in coming. A question of priestly law is raised to demonstrate that all activity is corrupted by lethargy. The offering of unacceptable sacrifices had made the whole nation unclean. On the other hand, blessings are assured from the Lord once the temple has been rebuilt. The question is, Can holy flesh (cf. Lev. 6:27) by contact make other articles holy? The answer is negative. But contact with the dead does impart uncleanness. To make an understandable analogy one might ask if a well man can infuse his health to others. The answer is, of course, negative, but all know that one sick man can spread disease to a whole community.

Despite the want of the past (Hag. 2:16, 17), since the temple is being reconstructed, God will now bless (2:19).

Oracle four was given the same day as oracle three and promises divine protection by Zerubbabel (2:20-23). The overthrowing of the nations is promised, but Zerubbabel, the Lord's servant, is chosen and will be as a signet. This is in marked contrast to the doom pronounced on the house of Jehoiachin (Jer. 22:24). Be the hidden import of this oracle what it may, we notice that the Messianic line is traced through Zerubbabel (Matt. 1:12; Luke 3:27).

The Influence of Haggai

The temple was completed by 516 B.C. (Ezra 6:15) and, though desecrated in the time of Antiochus, IV Epiphanes (168 B.C.), stood until it was replaced in the days of Herod the Great. (See A. Parrot, *The Temple in Jerusalem,* London: SCM Press, 1957). The book of Haggai was known to the writer of Ecclesiasticus 49:11 who includes Zerubbabel among "famous men" and calls him a "signet on the right hand." The Dead Sea community included this book among those it copied.

The writer of the epistle to the Hebrews furnishes the one clear echo from Haggai that is in the New Testament when he speaks of the "shaking of the heavens" (Hag. 2:6; Heb. 12:26-28) in contrast with the kingdom that cannot be shaken.

DISCUSSION

1. Can you find in the church today evidence of a spirit comparable to that faced by Haggai?
2. How do we arrive at dates that we assign to Old Testament figures?
3. What conditions did the returned exiles find in Jerusalem?
4. Do you believe Christians today are as concerned with God's work as with their own houses?
5. What questions concerning God's providence does the study of Haggai raise?
6. What do we learn about tasks and work from this prophet?
7. What verses in Haggai do you find most challenging?
8. What has Haggai to teach concerning ownership of the world's assets?
9. What lessons relevant to our day can you see in Haggai's discussion of evil?
10. Should one attribute a Messianic meaning to Old Testament passages wherever possible?

Chapter X

THE PROPHET ZECHARIAH

The Prophet

Zechariah, whose name means "He whom Jehovah remembers" (a name shared by 29 biblical figures), is one of the three writing prophets of the Persian Period and is a contemporary and co-laborer with Haggai in stirring the returned exiles to complete the temple. Zechariah's book is eleventh in the sequence of the minor prophets. Calling himself "the prophet" (*ha-nabi*; Zech. 1:1, 7), Zechariah introduces himself as the son of Berechiah and grandson of Iddo, the latter of whom is possibly the levitical Iddo who is mentioned in the list of returnees under Zerubbabel (Neh. 12:4, 16). Zechariah himself is listed among the priests who made that journey (Neh. 12:16). In Ezra (5:1; 6:14), Zechariah is merely called "son of Iddo," though it is likely that this is the looser use of "son" meaning descendant, which usage is also seen in Genesis 29:5.

The prophet, despite his being "son of Berechiah," is likely not the slain prophet of the Gospels (Matt. 23:35; Luke 11: 51), for that prophet is perhaps the Zechariah of 2 Chronicles 24:20. There is no evidence or tradition that the minor prophet suffered martyrdom.

Zechariah's activity, like that of Haggai, is dated by the years in the reign of Darius. There are three specific dates in the book which when transposed to our common chronology are: (1) The call to repentance, November 520 (1:1-6); (2) The night visions, February 519 (1:7–6:8); and (3) The response to the questions about fasting, December 518 (Chaps. 7-8). This means that Zechariah began his career two months later than Haggai, for his first oracle falls between the dates of the second and third oracles of Haggai (between Hag. 2:9 and 2:10). There is an overlap in time between the two prophets of one month. Zechariah continued in activity for two years. After that, we hear no more of him, not even at the dedication of the temple, though later legend made both him and Haggai to be founders of the Great Synagogue, a legendary body of leaders of the post-exilic period.

Historical Background

The return from exile began under Zerubbabel in 538 B.C. though many Jews remained in Babylon after that time. The temple had lain in ruins since its destruction by Nebuchadnezzar in 587 B.C. The returned exiles—perhaps mostly made up of young people with a sprinkling of old men—had begun reconstruction (Ezra 5:16; 3:1-6), but the effort had been blocked for 16 years by opposition from enemies. Times were bad. Haggai had stirred the people to resume activities in 520 B.C., but after two months' time had passed enthusiasm was low. At that point Zechariah added his voice to that of Haggai, urging the carrying of the project through to completion. The result of the two prophets' efforts was that the temple was completed in 516 B.C. (Ezra 6:15). We know no more of the post-exilic community for 59 years, at which time (457 B.C.) Ezra returned to Jerusalem to carry through reforms.

The Book

Section I:
A. The call to repentance (1:1-6). Reminding the people to learn the lesson of history—that God had been angry with their fathers—the prophet calls the people to return to God. The former prophets had called in vain, but God had accomplished his threats. The calamities of the exile had established that God's word abides forever.

B. The night visions (1:7—6:8). Three months after the preceding oracle (or in Feb. 519), two months after Haggai's last oracle, the prophet sees a series of visions, the explanations of which are furnished:

1. The rider on the red horse with red, sorrel, and white horses behind him. (1:7-17). These patrollers of the earth report that the earth is at rest, which seems bad news. "The shaking of the nations" (cf. Hag. 2:6, 7), which could restore Jerusalem to glory, is not visible. The angel of the vision, however, assures the prophet that after 70 years (cf. Jer. 25:11; 29:10) the Lord's pity is stirred and that Jerusalem will be rebuilt, while the heathen will be chastised.

2. The four horns and the four smiths (1:18-21). Horns, a symbol of power (cf. Micah 4:13), represent those powers that have scattered Judah. The smiths on the other hand are symbols of the destruction of those powers. The import of the vision is that there is no longer any opposition to the building of the Lord's house.

3. The man with the measuring line (2:1-13). The young man, about to lay out the walls of Jerusalem, is restrained since Jerusalem is to be inhabited as a city without walls. The Lord, who is "a wall of fire about her" and who will be glory in her midst, is to be her protection. The exiles still in Babylon are called upon to flee to Zion. Verse 12 is the only time in Scripture where Palestine is called "the holy land."

4. Joshua, a "brand plucked out of the burning" from the priesthood, in filthy garments, is accused by Satan as one might be accused before a court. In this condition he was unsuitable to offer acceptable sacrifices (3:1-10). Joshua was grandson of Seraiah, the last high priest who had ministered before the temple was destroyed. The outcome of the vision is that Satan is denounced and the filthy garments are removed and clean clothes substituted. The import of the vision is that the priesthood shall be cleansed and made acceptable for service. The oracle ends in a promise that God will send his

servant "the Branch" (cf. Isa. 11:1; Jer. 23:5; 33:15; Zech. 6:12) who, of course, is the Messiah.

5. The golden candlestick with seven lamps and two olive trees (4:1-14). The "two anointed ones" likely represent Zerubbabel and Joshua, the civil and religious heads of the community who are given assurance that the temple will be completed. Despite the difficulties now in the way, Zerubbabel, who had laid the foundation, will complete the capstone amidst applause. One should not despise the day of small things. The seven represent the all-seeing eye of God in his constant rule of earth. Success comes not by might and power, but by the Lord's spirit (4:6).

6. The flying scroll (5:1-4). The vision answers the question: How can crime be removed from the land? The scroll flies over the land and its curse destroys the houses of thieves and perjurers.

7. The woman sitting in an ephah (5:5-11). The woman, representing wickedness, sitting in a large dry measure (about seven gallons), is borne to Shinar where sin finds its natural home. With the temple rebuilt evil is to be removed from the land.

8. The four chariots from between the copper mountains go forth to patrol the earth (6:1-8). These seem to symbolize God's protecting providence. The earth is at peace under the control of God.

C. A coronation (6:9-15). Returnees from Babylon bring gold which is made into crowns (the Greek version has the singular "crown") and put on the head of Joshua. This act is a reminder of the advent of the "Branch."

D. Questions about fasting (7:1-7). A delegation from Bethel wants to know if the fasts now have relevance since the exile is over and work on the temple has progressed. The law demanded one day of fasting—that of the day of atonement—but fasts had sprung up commemorating the calamities (the burning of the temple, the murder of Gedaliah, the capture of the city, and the beginning of the siege). The prophet makes clear that it is not fasting, but obedience, justice, and kindness that is significant. The scattering of Judah was brought about by her disobedience (7:8-14).

E. Ten short oracles of encouragement introduced by "Thus saith the Lord" (8:1-23). These assure that the Lord will dwell in Zion and that prosperity is sure to come. In a beautiful picture the prophet sees Jerusalem as a city where boys and girls play in the streets and old men and old women sun themselves (8:4 f.).

Section II:

The second part of Zechariah contains three sections not clearly related to the problems of rebuilding the temple. The historical standpoint is different. The first person singular is not used as it is in the first part of the book. Two main divisions are introduced with the phrase, "An Oracle, the Word of the Lord" (9:1; 12:1), as also is Malachi. The material falls in the general type of literature known as apocalyptic.

A. Zechariah 9:1—10:12. After a preliminary denunciation of the neighboring nations whose land lies within the promised boundaries of the promised land (Gen. 15:18) and whose land is now to be incorporated into Judah, the prophet announces the triumph of Zion through her Messiah. The king comes riding on an ass (cf. 1 Kings 1:33, 38; Deut. 17:16) and his dominion is from sea to sea. Blessings come from the Lord, while idolatry is declared to be misleading. The Lord will signal and bring home the exiles with signs comparable to those at the time of the coming out of Egypt.

B. Zechariah 11:1-17. The good and the foolish shepherds. Lamenting the fate of the sheep, at the Lord's command the prophet takes charge of the flock and takes two staves which he names "graciousness" and "union," and in one month three shepherds are cut off (cf. Jer. 23:1-8; Ezek. 34; 37:24 f. for the shepherd as a figure of speech for the leader of God's people). No clue to the identity of these persons is available. The shepherd despairs of governing and asks for his wages. The price—thirty shekels of silver—the equivalent of the value of a Hebrew slave (cf. Exod. 21:32), is such a trifle that it is cast unto the potter; the stick union is broken to annul the brotherhood between Judah and Israel. The prophet is next ordered to become the worthless shepherd who in the end is stripped of his tools and punished (vss. 15-17).

C. Chapters 12-14 are made up of two sections, each of which deals with final events treated in an apocalyptic way. In the first, an attack by enemies upon Jerusalem results in victory for Judah through the Lord's aid. There is great mourning for one pierced. It is not possible to identify the historical events that lie back of this section. A fountain of cleansing is opened, and false prophets are cut off.

The second section announces the approach of the Day of the Lord with an assault on Zion, the intervention of Jehovah, and men fleeing from an earthquake. This earthquake is compared in severity to the one in the days of Uzziah (Amos 1:1; Zech. 14:5), though the latter occurred 400 years earlier than the times of the prophet Zechariah. The whole scene results in a transformed earth with all worshiping Jehovah and all things dedicated to his service.

Zechariah and the New Testament

Zechariah has exercised a greater influence upon the Messianic picture of the New Testament than any other minor prophet: (1) Further enlarging upon Jeremiah's promise of "the Branch of Jesse" (Jer. 23:5; 33:15; cf. 2 Sam. 7:12 f.), he points to the "Branch" (Zech. 3:8; 6:12). Though not directly quoted in the New Testament, the priestly king lies back of the conception of the Messiah in the Epistle to the Hebrews (cf. Ps. 110). (2) The king who rides upon the ass (Zech. 9:9; cf. Matt. 21:4 f.; John 12:15). (3) The betrayal (Zech. 11:12 f.; cf. Matt. 26:15; 27:9 f.); note the 30 pieces of silver and the potter's field. (4) Looking on him whom they have pierced (Zech. 12:10; John 19:37; Rev. 1:7). (5) Smite the shepherd (Zech. 13:7; cf. Matt. 26:31; Mark 14:27). (6) There is the king who reigns from sea to sea (9:10). (7) The fountain for cleansing (13:1).

Zechariah exercised other influences on the New Testament. His demand that everyone speak truth to his neighbor is echoed by Paul (Zech. 8:16; Eph. 4:25).

The reader of the book of Revelation may also find here the antecedent of certain pictures employed by that writer: (1) the four horsemen (Zech. 6:1-8); (2) the two olive trees (Zech. 4:3 ff.; Rev. 11:4); (3) the candlestick and seven eyes (Zech. 4:2-10; Rev. 1:12 f.).

Doctrines

It is to be noticed that in Zechariah angels as agents of revelation play a role that is unusual in the Old Testament. There are ranks of angels (1:11). This trend, perhaps beginning in the Persian period, can be further traced in the New Testament age, though there is evidence that it was opposed by the Sadducees.

"The Satan" appears as the accuser to bring men's failings to the attention of God (Zech. 3:1 f.; cf. 1 Chron. 21:1; Job 1:7 ff.; 2:1 ff.).

Attention is called to the oral law of the priests (7:2, 3). This developing law is later significant in Jesus' conflict with the Pharisees.

The Lord will be king over all the earth, and his name one (14:9). No better way could be found to describe the goal of our strivings in teaching and preaching the gospel than this verse from Zechariah.

DISCUSSION

1. What is the major activity with which the prophecy of Zechariah is concerned?

2. Summarize the picture of peace described by Zechariah.
3. What are the major differences between the two halves of the book?
4. What earlier prophecies do you find reflected in the prophecy of Zechariah?
5. What is the place of fasting as seen by Zechariah?
6. What are the major sins denounced by this prophet?
7. What are some examples of Zechariah's contribution to the Messianic hope? Are these literal or allegorical?
8. What participants in spiritual battles do we meet in Zechariah not previously encountered in the minor prophets? What is their role?
9. What are some of the influences of Zechariah on the New Testament?
10. What attitudes toward prophecy do you find reflected in Zechariah?

Chapter XI

THE PROPHET MALACHI

The Prophet

The twelfth and final prophet in the Book of the Twelve is Malachi. The personality of the prophet is entirely unknown; in fact, it is a debatable question that the prophet was actually named Malachi. The word means "my messenger" and is treated by the Septuagint as a common noun: "The burden of the Lord to Israel by the hand of his messenger" (Mal. 1:1) despite the fact that the LXX had already used the book title "Malachias." It is to be noticed, however, that in this version the possessive pronoun has been changed from the first to the third person. The Targum (the Aramaic translation of the Old Testament) has "my messenger whose name is Ezra the scribe." Jerome also accepted the tradition that ascribed the book to Ezra.

The Date

The time in which Malachi prophesied is determined by material within the book rather than from the opening lines of the book as has been true with earlier prophets. It is a time of careless priests (1:6–2:9), skepticism (3:14; 2:17), and of intermarriage (2:11-16). The temple is evidently completed and sacrifices are being offered (1:7-10). Judah is under a governor (1:8). Edom has been destroyed (1:1-5).

If we ask when these conditions existed, it seems that these problems are the same as those faced by Nehemiah (Neh. 5:14; 13:10-13). Tithing was also a matter of interest at that time (Neh. 10:37-39; cf. Mal. 3:8 f.). It is therefore likely that the prophet and Nehemiah were active at about the same time and it would be well to study Nehemiah as a background for Malachi. In other words, we are dealing with the Persian period of history and the governor alluded to is the Persian governor. The initial enthusiasm that characterized the returned exiles 70 years earlier has died out; the people are discouraged for the golden age has not dawned. The prophet writes to encourage the people by affirming that God still loves Israel and at the same time he expounds doctrines of the Lord's holiness and righteousness. Israel's sins have delayed her salvation.

The Style of the Book

The book of Malachi is written in a style unique in the prophets. Malachi makes abundant use of dialectic—a method that might be compared to that of the scribes: (1) An assertion is made. (2) A question that the assertion provoked is raised. This question is introduced by "Yet ye say" in eight occurrences (e.g., 2:14). (3) There is an elaboration of the original assertion with additional facts and illustrations. There are seven examples of the assertion-objection-rebuttal and these make up the fabric of the book.

1. I have loved you (1:2, 3).
2. You have despised my name (1:6, 7).
3. Judah has been faithless (2:10-16).
4. You have wearied the Lord with your words (2:17).
5. From the days of your fathers you have turned aside from my statutes (3:7).
6. You have robbed me (3:8).
7. Your words have been stout against me (3:13).

The Message

1. Surrounded by hostile neighbors and plagued by drought and bad crops, many question that God really loves Israel. The prophet answers that the love of God for Israel is to be

seen in the contrasting fates of Edom and Israel. Despite
the fact that they were brothers, Esau's country has been laid
waste and has remained so. The Edomites' plans for rebuilding are perpetually frustrated by the Lord. The Nabatean
Arabs had driven out the Edomites from their home lands.
The exact date of the invasion is unknown, but Nabateans
were already in Petra by 312 B.C. It is interesting to notice
that "hated" is used in this charge in a comparative way
to mean "loved less" as is true in numerous other biblical passages (Gen. 29:31; Deut. 21:15). It is further of interest to
notice the longstanding bitterness between Edom and Israel
dating all the way back to the prenatal struggle of their
ancestors (Gen. 25:22 f.); reflected in Edom's refusal to
permit Israel to pass through her land at the time of the
Wilderness Wandering (Num. 20:14 ff.); and further inten-
sified when Edom gloated over the fall of Judah to the Babylonians and aided in looting her (Obad. 10ff; Ps. 137:7; Lam.
4:21, 22). This oracle of Malachi against Edom should be
considered along with that of the book of Obadiah. The implied contrast is: though Israel has been exiled and though
prosperity has not come after the exile, she has survived the
experience and this is the evidence of God's love (1:2-5).
While the term "Lord of hosts" (Lord of Sabaoth) is by no
means unique in Scripture to Malachi, it is significant that
he uses the term more than 20 times.

2. Israel has despised God, not giving him the honor due
to a father or to a master. In particular the priests are guilty
of offering defective sacrifices rather than the unblemished
ones demanded by the law (cf. Deut. 15:21; Lev. 22:20-24).
The prophet challenges the people to see if the governor
would accept such gifts, insisting that God is held in higher
esteem among the heathen than among his own people (1:11).
The prophet utters a wish that someone would close the doors
of the temple rather than that such unworthy offerings be
made (1:10). Whether this means that the sacrifices of the
heathen are more acceptable than unworthy sacrifices offered
by Jews (cf. Luke 4:25 ff.); or whether it means that there are
proselytes; or that there are Jews apart from the temple who

worship (as for example those of Elephantine in upper Egypt in the fifth century B.C. where a Jewish temple is known to have existed and Jehovah was worshiped with animal sacrifices), this evaluation is unique with this prophet. A curse is on the man who offers a defective offering when he could do otherwise (1:14). The priests, chosen to give true instruction, are despised among the people for their negligence (2:1-9). This oracle of Malachi will never go out of date as long as the world has people who feel that though nothing is too good for our homes, just anything will do for the Lord.

3. Judah has been faithless in that Jewish wives have been divorced to marry the daughter of a strange god. Divorce is a breach of the covenant made with the wife of your youth. It is to be recalled that Ezra (Ezra 9:1 ff.) had to deal with the intermarriage problem. Malachi asserts that God desires "a godly offspring" (2:15). In the plainest statement on the divorce problem to be found in Scripture and despite the concession of Deuteronomy 24:1-4, God asserts, "I hate putting away." A monogamous relation is presupposed; the marriage bond is indissoluble. Here is stated most graphically the object of the religious home. In a world where at least one in three marriages ends in divorce and where the mixed marriage is common in which the effect upon the children is largely ignored, we would do well to listen to Malachi. The people are called to faithfulness (2:16).

One great thought of this book is: "Have we not all one Father, has not one God created us?" (2:10). In its context the passage upholds family loyalty; however, here lie seeds for the concepts both of the fatherhood of God and of the brotherhood of man.

4. A spirit of skepticism that insisted that the facts of life do not bear out that God is a God of justice is a weariness to the Lord (2:17). Not only so, but some suggest that God delights in evil doers. (This basic question of the prosperity of the wicked is often discussed in Scripture, cf. Ps. 73). The prophet answers that God will soon equalize the inequalities by judgment. The messenger will prepare his way. His coming

will purify the sons of Levi as one refines gold or silver.
Those who do not fear the Lord—sorcerers, adulterers, false
swearers—and those who oppress the fatherless and widows
will be punished (3:1-5). God does not change in his basic
opposition to sin nor in his basic trait of mercy (3:6).

5. There has been a continuous rebellion. If Israel will return to the Lord, he will return to her (3:6, 7).

6. Israel has robbed God by withholding tithes, which are
the annual contribution of one-tenth of the yield of the field
(Lev. 27:30 f.; Num. 18:21-32; Deut. 12:17 f.), and offerings,
which are the annual contribution to the priest (cf. Deut.
12:6, 11, 17). The result is that they have been cursed, but
the prophet promises that if the tithe is properly brought,
God will open his windows of blessing in prosperity so
conspicuous that they would become the envy of all nations
(Mal. 3:8-12). Notice that the promised blessing is material
as was also true of that made in Deuteronomy 28:1, 2, 12 for
obedience. Here is a promise that may well be compared with
that later made by Paul to the faithful giver (2 Cor. 9:10).

7. Further evidence of skepticism is seen in those who say
that it is vain to serve the Lord (Mal. 3:14). Though the wheat
and tares now grow together, the prophet answers this accusation by pointing to the coming blessing for the righteous
who are the Lord's special possession (cf. Exod. 19:5) on the
day in which he acts. God has his book of remembrance;
those written there will be spared as a man spares his son
(Mal. 3:13-18). But the coming of the Day of the Lord will
consume the wicked root and branch (4:1-3). Unlike in Amos
and some other early prophets, the Day of the Lord in Malachi seems to be the terminus of history. In contrast with the
fate of the wicked, to the righteous the coming of that day
will be as the rising of the sun after a long, dark night. In the
face of this threatened day, the prophet issues a call to remember the statutes of Moses (4:4) and promises that Elijah, the prophet, will be sent to turn the hearts of the fathers
to the children and vice versa before that day, lest the Lord
come and smite the earth with a curse (4:5).

The Messianic Element

Two passages in Malachi, traditionally interpreted in a Messianic way, should be carefully looked at:

1. Malachi 1:11: "For from the rising of the sun to its setting my name shall be great among the Gentiles. . ." The practice of supplying the future of the verb "to be" three times in this verse has made it into a Messianic passage. Since, however, the original does not express the verb, the present tense could just as well be supplied as has been done in the Revised Standard Version and certain other English versions.

2. Malachi 4:2: "The sun of righteousness shall arise with healing in its wings." At least as early as the time of Coverdale (1535), the sun of righteousness was understood to be Jesus. Coverdale renders the phrase "Sonne of Righteousness." This interpretation is continued in the "Translators to the Readers" of the King James Version: "But when the fullness of time drew near, that Sunne of righteousness, the Son of God should come into the world." This is a very doubtful interpretation since Hebrew uses a feminine pronoun "her wings" to agree with sun (*shemesh*) which is a feminine noun in Hebrew.

A more authentic Messianic element is to be seen in the promise of the messenger who prepares the way (3:1). This figure is also called Elijah the prophet (4:5). It will be remembered that Elijah was the single one among the prophets who did not die. This idea of a final and powerful appeal to be made before the last day is unique with this prophet. This expectation was quoted by Jesus as well as by the Gospel writers and applied to John the Baptist (Matt. 11:10; Mark 1:2; Luke 7:27 f.).

Malachi in the New Testament

1. Paul appealed to Malachi's assertion: "Jacob have I loved but Esau have I hated" to establish the election by the Lord (Rom. 9:13; Mal. 1:2, 3).

2. The Messenger to come (Mal. 3:1; Matt. 11:10). A New Testament passage (Mark 1:2) combines the statement from Malachi with Isaiah 40:3.
3. Elijah the prophet (Mal. 4:5 f.; Matt. 11:14).

Sins Denounced in Malachi

1. Moral offenses: adultery, perjury, oppression (3:5).
2. Divorce (2:16; cf. Mark 10:5 ff.).
3. Cultic abuses (1:8).
4. Skepticism, which says that there is no point in living the good life (3:14 f.).
5. Unworthy priests (2:7-9).
6. Robbing God (3:8, 9).

DISCUSSION

1. Compare the phrases expressing religious indifference used by Malachi and those used by other prophets.
2. What contribution has Malachi to make to the marriage-divorce question? Compare it with New Testament teaching.
3. In the light of Malachi's teaching, what conclusions must be drawn concerning the quality of offerings made to the Lord? Is robbery a common practice?
4. What has Malachi to teach about half-hearted worship?
5. What ideas about the brotherhood of man are suggested by this prophet?
6. What suggestions about the purposes of the godly home may be drawn from Malachi?
7. Is it possible that Malachi affirms that pagan worship is more acceptable than that of the temple?
8. What lessons about religious leadership are to be learned from Malachi?
9. What material can you assemble about the book of life?
10. What is Malachi's contribution to the expectation of a Messianic age?

Chapter XII

THE PROPHET OBADIAH

The Prophet

Obadiah, the fourth in the sequence of the minor prophets, is unknown other than from his book. Obadiah's name means "servant of the Lord." Despite the fact that there are 13 men with this name in the Old Testament, no valid reason can be given for identifying the prophet with any of them. Three characters have been nominated at various times: The Talmud (*T. B. Sanhedrin* 39b) suggests that the prophet is to be identified with Ahab's servant (1 Kings 18:3 f.). Pseudo-Epiphanius, *The Lives of the Prophets,* identifies him with Ahaziah's captain (2 Kings 1:13-15). Still others would make him a servant of Jehoshaphat (2 Chron. 17:7); but none of these cases are conclusive. We have no material from which to draw a precise picture of the life and personality of the prophet.

Not even the date of the prophet can be determined with definiteness. Guesses have ranged from 850 B.C.—the campaign of Shishak against Judah (1 Kings 14:25)—on down to 312 B.C. when Antigonus ordered an expedition against the Arabs that were in possession of Edom. The place of the book in the minor prophets may suggest an early date, but other considerations also must be weighed. Its position may be due to the fact that Amos 9:12 also predicts the fate of Edom. The point of departure for dating the book is ordinarily an effort to date the calamity that Jerusalem has suffered which is reflected in the book. The fact, however, that Jerusalem suffered at least four times—(1) Shishak's campaign (1 Kings 14:25, 26; 2 Chron. 12:1-12); (2) the Arabians and the Philistines (2

Chron. 21:16, 17; (3) the defeat of Amaziah (2 Kings 14:
8-14; 2 Chron. 25:17-24); and (4) Nebuchadnezzar in 586
B.C.—makes the arguments on date less than conclusive.
There is nothing in the book to furnish a convincing, definite picture of the prophet's life and times. Despite all cases
made, the calamity here spoken of can hardly be other than
that brought about by Nebuchadnezzar in 586 B.C. (cf. Obad.
20).

The Book

The book of Obadiah with its 21 verses is the shortest book
in the Hebrew Bible. Like Joel, Jonah, Nahum, Habakkuk,
and Malachi it has no superscription explaining when it was
composed. Like the book of Nahum (cf. Habakkuk and
Isaiah where the verb "to see" occurs at the beginning of the
book), it is called a vision (Obad. 1).

Obadiah is one of the seven Old Testament books (Nahum,
Ezra, Nehemiah, Esther, Song of Songs, Ecclesiastes, and
Obadiah) that are not quoted or echoed in the New Testament; however, the twelve prophets were already recognized
in Judaism earlier than the New Testament period.

Obadiah is an oracle on a foreign nation rather than a
denunciation of Judah. Its general message with its two parts
is not difficult to summarize and to grasp:

1. Obadiah 1-14. In spite of her inaccessible mountain shel-
ters and her proverbial wisdom, Edom will be invaded by
disloyal allies and her people driven out. The prophet sees
the calamity as a divine punishment for Edom's cruelties
toward Israel.

2. Obadiah 15-21. A prediction of the Day of the Lord
with the restoration and victory of Israel.

It is to be noticed that the prophet has no denunciation of
sin for Israel, no call to righteousness, and no expression of
mercy. His burden is entirely devoted to the doom of Edom.
Its purpose seems to be not to warn the Edomites, but to
comfort the Israelites.

Literary Relations

It is obvious to the student that there is a marked similarity between the oracle on Edom found in Jeremiah 49:7-16 and that found in Obadiah 1-9. Many have felt that Obadiah borrowed his material from Jeremiah. A careful look at the context of the proverb common to Obadiah 8 and Jeremiah 49:7 will seem to support, however, that the two writers are independent of each other.

There is also a similarity between numerous phrases found in Joel 3 and Obadiah: "because of violence" (Joel 3:19; Obad. 10); "your deeds shall return on your own head" (Joel 3:4-7; Obad. 15); "the day of the Lord is near" (Joel 1:15; 2:1; 3:14; Obad. 15); "in Mt. Zion there shall be those that escape" (Joel 2:32; Obad. 17); and "Zion shall be holy" (Joel 3:17; Obad. 17).

Edom and Israel

The written records and monuments of the Edomites have perished. Our sources of information concerning them are the Old Testament, the records of the neighbors of Edom, and archaeological exploration.

Edom occupied a narrow mountainous strip of territory (mountain peaks range up to 5,700 feet) about 100 by 20 miles in dimensions, located on the eastern side of the Palestinian rift valley. This territory stretches from the Brook Zared (today this is Wadi el Hesa) to the Gulf of Aqabah. It is bounded on the east by the desert. Edom means "the red region" which name is probably to be connected with the red rocks that are abundant in the territory. Seir (Gen. 32:3; Deut. 2:1, 5; Judg. 5:4) is another biblical name for the Edomite region and refers to the mountain range that runs north and south through its entire length. Once heavily wooded, this region has now been almost completely deforested. In the Old Tesament Sela (perhaps Petra), Teman (modern Tawilan), and Bosrah (modern Buseirah) were its fortified citadels. The present-day visitor to Petra, which

Burgon called "a rose red city—half as old as time," gets some taste of the ruggedness of this land. The buildings to be seen date from the Roman period, but the site itself is much older. One enters Petra by the Sik, a narrow canyon more than a mile in length with vertical walls often not more than 30 feet apart. Here a few men could hold off an entire army. The deep colored sandstone cliffs which change colors by the hour are most impressive. Out of these cliffs the Nabateans carved their temples. It is one of the most impressive sights in the world. Petra became a caravan city that had few fears of successful attack and lost its significance only when new routes took trade via Palmyra, far to the north.

It is interesting to notice that Edomite religion is not discussed or denounced in the Old Testament. Nothing is said about Edomite gods, though this is not to be interpreted that they had none. From external sources it may be deduced that they worshiped deities: Hadad, Jaush, and perhaps even Edom, itself, may be the name of a deity. The language of Edom was probably a dialect related to Hebrew. The government was monarchial (cf. Gen. 36:31-39).

The conflicts between Israel and Edom are traced in the Old Testament all the way back to a prenatal struggle of the ancestors Jacob and Esau (Gen. 25:22 f.). At the same time, it is recognized that fundamentally the two peoples are "brethren." The Edomite was not to be abhorred and Israel was forbidden to take Edom's territory (Deut. 23:7; 2:5-8) despite the fact that Edom refused Israel passage at the time of the Wilderness Wandering (Num. 20:14 ff.). The Edomite was to be permitted to enter the congregation after three generations (Deut. 23:8). Nevertheless, Edom's "anger tore perpetually and he kept his wrath forever" (Amos 1:11).

The major causes of conflict were likely economic. The trade route from south Arabia, as well as sea trade, converged at Aqabah and passed on "the King's highway" through Edomite territory (cf. 1 Kings 9:26-28; 10:22; 22:47, 48). It was also in this district and to the west of the rift valley that the copper industry of ancient Palestine was to be found. The mining industry contributed greatly to Edomite wealth. David conquered the territory (2 Sam. 8:14) and Solomon exploited its advantages. There are echoes of later revolts of Edom during the period of the kings (1 Kings 11: 14-22; 2 Kings 8:20-22). It would appear that Assyrian and Bablylonian sovereignty extended to Edom as well as to Israel.

It was, however, the behaviour of Edom during the Babylonian period that seems to have been remembered most bitterly. Edomites joined the Babylonian forces in the siege and capture of Judah (586 B.C.) and then expanded into the vacuum created by the fall of Judah (Ps. 137:7; Ezek. 35:1-15). Some Judeans attempted to find temporary refuge among the Edomites but were unwelcome there (Jer. 40:11).

By the time the book of Malachi was written, Edom had suffered a severe defeat (Mal. 1:2-5). At an undetermined period Nabatean Arabs took over the territory of Edom. By 312 B.C. it was called Idumaea (Diodorus Siculus xix.94). Numerous Nabatean remains are to be seen in this area as well as in south Judah. During the Maccabean period (ca. 120 B.C.) the Nabateans were subjected to Judaism by John Hyrcanus (Josephus, Ant., 13.9.1). This episode may meet the demands for a second devastation of the territory mentioned by the prophet. The Idumaeans supplied history with Herod who became king of the Jews. The territory came under Roman domination during the Roman period.

The long history of the struggle between Israel and Edom has many echoes in biblical literature. These passages may well be studied as a background for Obadiah's oracle: Amos 1:11, 12; Isa. 34:5 ff.; 63:1-6; Jer. 49:7-22; Ezek. 25:12-14; 35:1 ff.; Lam. 4:21 f.; Joel 3:19; Mal. 1:2-5; Ecclus. 50:25, 26. Obadiah, however, is the climax of hatred of all of these oracles.

The Message

In moving poetic imagery, the poet presents the downfall of Edom. A messenger is sent from the Lord among the nations to announce the doom. First, attention is drawn to

Edom's confident pride. It is a false trust that she has in her mountain strongholds. She trusts in Sela (which some have thought we should identify with Petra, for Petra means rock in Greek as Sela means rock in Hebrew) and she says, "Who will bring me down?" The prophet sees the doom as the working of the Lord. He does not threaten destruction from Assyria, Babylon, Greece, or Rome, but her doom is from the Lord. Even though Edom soar like the eagle and set her nest among the stars, "I will bring you down says the Lord." Nevertheless, the Lord uses tools. He uses her unfaithful allies to accomplish this task. Though the Hebrew verbs of the book are often in the perfect tense, it is likely that they are prophetic perfects expressing the certain future, though it must be admitted that one is not always certain that the prophet is not describing the past.

The extent of the destruction is presented in a series of figures: Thieves would only steal sufficient to satisfy themselves while leaving the remainder behind. Changing the figure, grape gatherers would leave some gleanings (cf. Deut. 24:21; Lev. 19:9, 10), but Esau has been thoroughly pillaged. Her allies in whom she trusted have now turned upon her and have plundered her. Her wise men have failed her (cf. Job 15:1, 18 for her reputation for wisdom). Her various advantages have been unable to deliver her. However, the prophet makes clear that the whole affair is the Lord's doing in order to cut off Esau.

Beyond the pride above mentioned, what is the sin of Edom? It is a manifest display of lack of brotherliness. She refused to aid when Judah was plundered; rather, she stood by and gloated over the misfortune. Already in the Old Testament, rejoicing at calamity is considered a sin (Prov. 17:5; Job 31:29). But not only did Edom pass by on the other side as did the Levite and the priest in the New Testament story (Luke 10:31 ff.), but she joined in with the attackers to loot (Obad. 13) and stood at the parting of the ways to cut off refugees (vs. 14). This day is called "the day of your brother" (vs. 12) as earlier in the Old Testament "the day of Midian" is the day of its doom (Isa. 9:4) or "his day" for the wicked

is the day of facing God (Ps. 37:13; cf. Job 18:20). The
threat of the prophet is that as Edom has done, it shall be
done to her. Her chickens will surely come home to roost
(Obad. 15).

A second portion of the book presents the Day of the Lord
in an apocalyptic way in which Edom is made to drink the
cup of God's wrath. Drinking the cup of wrath as a figure of
doom develops an idea seen in Jeremiah 25:15 ff. and Psalm
75:8. This figure is continued in the New Testament (John
18:11; Rev. 14:10). Here, as elsewhere in the prophets, the
Day of the Lord is a day within history after which history
will continue. The contrasting fates of the house of Jacob
and Esau are presented. The house of Jacob shall burn Esau
as stubble and there will be no survivor for Esau. His future
is entirely black.

In contrast, the prophet promises a return of exiles—both
Judah and Joseph—to possess the land from Phoenicia to the
Mount of Esau as well as the territory of Gilead. Finally, in a
most optimistic moment the prophet asserts "the Kingdom
shall be the Lord's."

Great Lessons of the Prophet

John Calvin correctly remarked that Obadiah was shorter
and did not suggest as many sermons as the longer prophets;
nevertheless, lessons are not absent.

Obadiah is a standing rebuke to the spirit who prefers not
to become involved in the problems of others, but it is even
more a rebuke to him who finds a sadistic joy in the mis-
fortunes of another.

The prophet makes quite clear that the idea of the in-
vulnerability of nations is a delusion.

One should not overlook the firm faith of this prophet in
divine providence which will work out its purpose in history
to give Edom its due but whose final outcome shall be the
Kingdom of God.

DISCUSSION

1. How is the spirit of vengeance displayed in Obadiah to be dealt with by the Christian?
2. Does Obadiah have anything to say to the man who, in the presence of calamity, does not want to get involved?
3. What is Obadiah's outlook on the final outcome of history?
4. What has Obadiah to say to a militaristic age?
5. Give briefly the high points in the relations of Israel and Edom.
6. Discuss the themes of Obadiah in the light of "love your enemies."
7. What is Obadiah's teaching concerning the means of God's operation in history?
8. Contrast the dealings of God with Edom and Israel in the Old Testament.
9. What has the Bible to teach about holding grudges?
10. Contrast the teaching of Obadiah on pride and that found elsewhere in the Old Testament.

Chapter XIII

THE PROPHET JOEL

The Times of the Prophet

The book of the prophet Joel is the second in sequence of the minor prophets. Twelve men in the Bible bear the name Joel which name means "Jehovah is God"; however, there is no valid reason for connecting the others with the prophet. Actually, we know nothing reliable about the prophet beyond that material contained in his book. His father, Pethuel (Joel 1:1), is otherwise unknown. Joel, as the content of his book indicates, is obviously a prophet of Judah.

Pseudo-Epiphanius, *The Lives of the Prophets,* informs us that the prophet was originally from the land belonging to the tribe of Reuben and that he was buried in Bethmeon. This is doubtless a guess based on 1 Chronicles 5:4 and need not be taken seriously.

The ministry and the book of Joel lack definite dates. Conjectures range over four centuries, with each conjecture based on debatable presuppositions. It is usually thought that Joel must be either quite early or quite late. Those who would date Joel in the pre-exilic period—often as early as the ninth century B.C. to make him among the earliest prophets—point out that the enemies dealt with in the book are the Philistines, Phoenicians, Egyptians, and Edomites rather than those of the exilic period. Furthermore there is no reference either to Assyria, which emerged as a power as early as 760 B.C., or to Babylon, which followed but which had fallen out of the picture by 537 B.C. It might also be argued that the early position in the sequence of the prophets indicates that ancient tradition took it to be an early book.

Those of contrary mind may argue that neither of these

points is conclusive, for Obadiah, though it seems to be post-exilic, also is placed early in sequence of the prophetic books. Date does not always seem to be the determinative factor in the place of a book. The book differs greatly in style from the early prophets, especially in its eschatology. This argument, however, which has been heavily depended upon for dating, is now weakening as there is considerable tendency to date the rise of eschatological beliefs in Israel considerably earlier than formerly was true. Often now it is admitted that some eschatology may precede prophecy.

The case for a post-exilic book points out that the Northern Kingdom is not mentioned. Israel is now only Judah. Elders and priests are the authorities in Jerusalem; there is no king mentioned. Echoes of plundering of the temple (Joel 3:5); "scattering among the nations" (3:2); and sale of slaves to the Greeks (3:6) are all claimed to be evidences of late date. It is also to be noticed that the religious conditions of the earlier period are not reflected. The "high place" and the tendency to idolatry go unmentioned. No prophet dwells so little upon moral considerations.

Those who rebut to this case point out that the phrase "restore the fortunes" is in Amos 9:14 and Hosea 6:11 so that the threat of plundering and exile need not reflect a late date. Though Greeks are not mentioned in Scripture before Ezekiel 27:13, 19 (*Javan* in Hebrew is Greece), they are mentioned early by Sargon and in the Tell Amarna letters; hence this item also is not conclusive for a late date.

The literary relationship of Joel to other prophets is a part of the argument. It is estimated that 27 out of the 73 verses are paralleled in other prophets. We have already called attention to some of these in studying Obadiah, but there are some others:

1:15	—	Isa. 13:6
2:2	—	Zeph. 1:15
2:3	—	Isa. 51:3; Ezek. 36:35
2:10	—	Isa. 13:10
2:32	—	Obad. 17

          3:10 — Isa. 2:4; Micah 4:3
          3:16 — Amos 1:2; Isa. 13:13
          3:17 — Ezek. 36:11; Isa. 52:1; Obad. 17
                   Nah. 1:15
          3:18 — Amos 9:13

Those who are convinced that Joel is early argue that Joel is used by those who came after, and as might be expected, those who believe that Joel is late argue the converse. Thus the discussion goes on in uncertainty with the majority of recent books tending toward placing Joel late among the prophets.

The Book

Joel was stimulated by a particularly severe locust plague to explain its significance and to call his people to repentance. The book, which has sometimes been called "the locust plague and what it teaches," seems to be more an episode than a report of a long prophetic career. The 73 verses are divided into four chapters in the Hebrew Bible, but are only three (Chaps. 2 and 3 are combined into one) in the other versions including English. The book also has three major sections:

1. The locust plague and drought call the people to repentance (1:1–2:27).

2. The Day of the Lord, heralded by the outpouring of the Spirit (2:28–3:16).

3. The glorious future of Judah and Jerusalem (3:17-21).

The Locusts

A plague of locusts of unparalleled magnitude furnishes the occasion of Joel's prophecy (cf. Amos 7:1, 2). It is such that those who have lived previously have not seen its parallel (1:2) and it will be spoken of in generations to come (1:3). Biblical Hebrew has 12 terms for various varieties of locusts. Four of them, *Gazam, Arbeh, Yeleg,* and *Chasil*—i.e. cutting, swarming, hopping, and destroying—are found here and it is sometimes thought that they describe successive stages of the same plague, though it is admitted that they are not listed in the same order in Joel 1:4 and Joel 2:25.

The plague is not evaluated from its economic impact so much as from its religious significance. The prophet seizes the opportunity to call various classes of society who have been adversely affected to repentance. The supply of wine is cut off from the drunkards (1:10), the farmers wail because of the failure of crops (1:11), priests wail because there are inadequate supplies for offerings (1:9, 13). It should especially be noticed that Joel is interested in ritual. Even the bride and bridegroom, usually exempt from public obligations (Deut. 24:5), are called upon to join in (2:16).

In two largely parallel sections Joel describes the locusts (1:4-20; 2:3-11). In most graphic pictures the poet shows them as they lay waste the vine and strip off bark from the trees (1:7). Fields are waste and oil and wine fail (1:10). With the failure of supplies, there is little way to propitiate the Lord. Before the locusts it was like the garden of Eden, but after them there is a desolate wilderness (2:3).

This plague is coupled together with a drought that leaves the seed shriveling under the clods (1:17) and the beasts dismayed for lack of pasture. The pasture has been burned as with fire and brooks are dry (1:18-20).

Joel describes the advance of the locusts as though they were war horses, rumbling like chariots. The sound is as the sound of the crackling of a flame of fire (2:5). Or again they are as an army marching on its way, each without jostling the other, scaling the wall and entering the house (2:4-9). The student would do well to read the description of the plague of 1915 in which the locusts also came from the north as they do in Joel (John D. Whiting, "Jerusalem's Locust Plague," *National Geographic* XXVIII [1915], 511-550).

It is readily admitted that the allegorists have attempted to make the locusts into human invaders: Assyrians, Chaldeans, Macedonians, and Romans. Others have made a moral allegory: anger, lust, vainglory, and impatience. Still others have attempted to make them into apocalyptic monsters. Though it is a debatable question whether the locusts are to be understood literally or as apocalyptic creatures, in this lesson we consider them to be a real locust plague contemporary with the prophet. The prophet is not predicting that the surrounding nations would invade the land after the manner of a plague of locusts.

The Day of the Lord

Joel sees the approach of the locusts as the approach of the Day of the Lord. We have met the concept of the Day of the Lord in Amos, Zephaniah, and Malachi, but here it is an agricultural phenomenon rather than a political one. It is not a day of gladness. Joel announces that it comes as destruction from the Almighty (1:15). The locusts are the Lord's devouring army. "The Day of the Lord is great and very terrible; who can endure it?" (2:11). The phrase is five times in Joel (1:15; 2:1, 11, 31; 3:14). For the Day of the Lord in other prophets, see Amos 5:18 ff.; Isaiah 2:12; 13:6, 9 f.; Zephaniah 1:14 f.; Jeremiah 46:10; Ezekiel 30:2 f.; Obadiah 15; Zechariah 14:1; Malachi 4:5.

Repent!

It is in the face of this calamity that Joel urges the calling of a national assembly for repentance. Uniquely, he does not mention and condemn specific sins either private or national, but calls for rending of hearts as a contrast to external show of torn garments (2:12, 13). It was no washing-of-the-outside-of-the-cup affair. Since the Lord is merciful, who knows but that he may relent (2:14). The priests are called upon to appeal to the Lord's "tender nerve": "Spare thy people, O Lord, and make not thy heritage a reproach and a by-word among the nations."

The Goodness of God

Presupposing repentance on the part of the people, the Lord promises a removal of the locusts (2:20); a restoral of oil and wine (2:19); and ample rain in its seasons (2:23). The years of the locusts will be restored (2:25), and there shall be plenty (2:26, 27).

There will be an outpouring of the Spirit with portents in heaven and on earth with salvation for those who call on the name of the Lord (2:28-32).

The Day of the Lord for the Nations

In the third section of his book the prophet summons the nations into the valley of Jehoshaphat, an unknown geographical location, but which very name contains a pun meaning "Jehovah judges" (3:12). Their wickedness is great (3:13). The nations are judged for having scattered the Lord's people (3:2, 3). The Phoenicians and Philistines are denounced for plundering the Lord's people—particularly for the sale of slaves to the Greeks (3:6). In measure-for-measure punishment, their sons will be sold to the Sabeans (3:8).

It is a harvest, not of grain, but of destruction. No hope of a remnant is extended. The nations are called upon to convert their weapons of peace into weapons of war (3:9, 10; cf. Isa. 2:4 and Micah 4:3), but it really is all in vain for it is the Lord they face in the valley of decision, which is a further pun on Jehoshaphat. The prophet promises desolation to Egypt and Edom, but a brilliant future awaits Judah as the Lord dwells in Zion (3:19-21).

Joel and the New Testament

The book of Joel is directly appealed to in the New Testament in two passages:

1. It was to Joel that Peter appealed to explain the outpouring of the Spirit on Pentecost (Acts 2:17-21; cf. Joel 2:28-32; Num. 11:29).

2. Paul used the phrase, "Whoever calls on the name of the Lord shall be saved" (Rom. 10:13; Joel 2:32).

There are echoes of the book, particularly in the book of Revelation. The moon turned to blood (Joel 2:31; Rev. 6:12); the description of the Day of the Lord (Joel 2:10; cf. Matt. 24:29; Mark 13:24; Luke 21:25); the judgment as a harvest (Joel 3:13; Matt. 13:39; Rev. 14:17 ff.); and treading the winepress as a symbol of judgment (Joel 3:13; cf. Rev. 14:20; 19:15; Isa. 63:3). The locusts of 2:1-11 may be echoed in Revelation 9:3-11.

DISCUSSION

1. What traits of God do you see most plainly presented in Joel?
2. What are the chief duties of men that are emphasized?
3. What is the cause of calamity as seen by Joel? Can we subscribe to this idea?
4. Is the Day of the Lord a day within history or the terminus of history?
5. What is involved in repentance as seen by Joel?
6. Should Joel be interpreted literally or allegorically?
7. What are the chief questions involved in dating Joel?
8. What part did external stimuli play in prophetic revelation?
9. Why is Joel sometimes called the prophet of Pentecost?
10. What is the purpose of fasting?